Applying Social Psychology

SAGE SOCIAL PSYCHOLOGY PROGRAMME

Senior Consultant Editor

Michael A. Hogg (Claremont Graduate University, USA)

Consultant Editors

Richard E, Petty (Ohio State University USA)
Marilynn B. Brewer (Ohio State University USA)
John M. Levine (University of Pittsburgh USA)
Stephen Reicher (St. Andrews University UK)
Vincent Yzerbet (Université Catholique de Louvain Belgium)

SAGE Publications is pleased to announce the launch of a new, international programme of titles in social psychology – both textbook and reference – brought together by a team of consultant editors led by Michael A. Hogg: the **SAGE Social Psychology Programme**. Featuring books written or edited by world-leading scholars (or younger academics 'on the rise') and infused with the latest research in the field, the programme is intended to be a self-contained, comprehensive resource that meets all the educational needs of a social psychology programme beyond introductory level.

The remit of the **SAGE Social Psychology Programme** has both breadth and depth. Student textbooks are written by leading and experienced scholars in a style that is carefully crafted to be stimulating, engaging and accessible. They are schoarly, comprehensive and up-to-date, and boast the appropriate pedagogical devices and supplements – thus making them appropriate to build courses around at a variety of levels. Reference works, including Handbooks and Encyclopaedias, survey the landscape with an even broader sweep and should become benchmark volumes for years to come.

Current and forthcoming titles include:

1. **Understanding Social Psychology across Cultures** – Peter Smith (*University of Sussex, UK*), Michael Bond (*Chinese University of Hong Kong, China*) & Ciğdem Kağitçibasi (*Koc University, Istanbul, Turkey*)
   Published – December 2005
2. **Cognitive Dissonance: 50 Years of a Classic Theory** – Joel Cooper (*Princeton University, USA*)
   Publication date: March 2007
3. **The SAGE Handbook of Social Psychology: Concise Student Edition** – Michael A. Hogg (*Claremont Graduate University, USA*) & Joel Cooper (*Princeton University, USA*)
   Publication date: March 2007
4. **The Encyclopedia of Social Psychology: 3 Volumes** – Roy F. Baumeister (*Florida State University, USA*) & Kathleen D. Vohs (*University of Minnesota, USA*)
   Publication date: September 2007

Applying Social Psychology

From Problems to Solutions

Abraham P. Buunk and
Mark Van Vugt

SAGE Publications
Los Angeles • London • New Delhi • Singapore

First published 2008

SAGE Publications Ltd
1 Oliver's Yard
55 City Road
London EC1Y 1SP

SAGE Publications Inc.
2455 Teller Road
Thousand Oaks, California 91320

SAGE Publications India Pvt Ltd
B 1/I 1 Mohan Cooperative Industrial Area
Mathura Road
New Delhi 110 044

SAGE Publications Asia-Pacific Pte Ltd
33 Pekin Street #02-01
Far East Square
Singapore 048763

Library of Congress Control Number: 2007926759

British Library Cataloguing in Publication data

A catalogue record for this book is available from
the British Library

ISBN 978-1-4129-0282-3
ISBN 978-1-4129-0283-0 (pbk)

Typeset by C&M Digitals (P) Ltd, Chennai, India
Printed in Great Britain by The Cromwell Press Ltd, Trowbridge, Wiltshire
Printed on paper from sustainable resources

To Yvonne A.B. Werkhoven, a truly applied social
psychologist. (APB)

To Hannie, my parents Leo and Corrie, my son Jamie and to
all applied researchers and their contributions. (MVV)

CONTENTS

ABOUT THE AUTHORS

Abraham (Bram) P. Buunk has been since 2005 Academy Professor in Evolutionary Social Psychology at the University of Groningen on behalf of the Royal Netherlands Academy of Arts and Sciences. His main current interest is the application of evolutionary theorizing to human social behaviour. He has published widely on applied topics, including professional burnout, jealousy, absenteeism, AIDS-prevention, loneliness, depression, marital satisfaction, well-being among the elderly, and coping with cancer. He was a co-editor of *Health, coping and well-being: Perspectives from social comparison theory* (Erlbaum, 1997), and *Solidarity and Prosocial Behaviour* (Springer, 2006). He has served on scientific boards for the Dutch Cancer Foundation (NKB-KWF), and the Dutch AIDS Foundation. Currently he is a member of the Programme Committee on Evolution and Behaviour of the Netherlands Organization for Scientific Research (NWO).

Mark Van Vugt is Professor of Social Psychology at the University of Kent at Canterbury. He did his undergraduate degree at the University of Groningen and his PhD at the University of Maastricht in the Netherlands. He has published widely on topics in social and applied psychology, including leadership, social dilemmas, altruism and cooperation, social identity, environmental conservation, transport and water management. He is the chief editor of *Cooperation in modern society: Promoting the welfare of communities, states, and organizations* (Routledge, 2000). He is a fellow of the British Academy and sits on the editorial board of several journals in social psychology.

PREFACE

One of the wonderful experiences in life is that of having a problem and calling an expert, who walks in, takes a look, makes reassuring noises, goes to work and hey presto, your central heating system starts spreading comfort and happiness again. When I returned to academia after a stint as management consultant I realized looking back that I might have fallen somewhat short in providing clients with these wonderful experiences.

Reflecting on what I had actually been using of the knowledge and tools acquired during my training as a social psychologist, I realized that the tools had come in handy but that the application of knowledge/theories hardly figured prominently. I was well equipped to interview people, construct questionnaires and surveys and arrive at an adequate analysis of problems. Yet when it came to providing solutions it seemed I had been mainly relying on common sense combined with the usual role of process consultant. This is a bit like your central heating engineer presenting you with, admittedly, a fine diagnosis of the problem and then offering to hold your hand while you wrestle with finding a way of getting the system to deliver some heat again.

People, groups and organizations are obviously much more complex than the simple systems that keep the house operating: all the more reason to train future practitioners in using the theories and accumulated bodies of knowledge available. Extensive screening of the literature at the time did not throw up the desired textbook/training manual. So I started out developing my own course, which after the usual evolutionary developments has now taken shape as the PATH (Problem-Analysis-Test-Help) model presented in this book.

At first sight this model looks the same as every other problem-solving course. The essential differences the PATH model introduces are twofold:

1. from the very beginning it stresses using theories (plural) that might help to define and delineate the problem and, in the problem-solving phase suggests solutions that consequently have a solid foundation in theory and research; 2. in finding solutions, it examines factors that have a realistic chance of being changed.

In addition to making better use of the available knowledge, the PATH model has the happy side-effect that practising social psychologists are better protected against confusing themselves or their clients.

When in later life I was in charge of a large organization, using consultants from time to time, I was often struck by the difference between the business school alumni and social/organizational psychologists. The first category were strong on analysis and practical solutions they claimed had worked for others. The psychologists were strong on analysis and nearly always flavoured their solutions with a whiff of how things ought to be. Both groups succeeded in keeping any reference to research and theory well out of sight. This is actually good practice in an applied setting: the average manager/client does not always want to be bothered with academic trivia.

Unfortunately, I am pretty confident that empirically-based theories only played a marginal role for both business school alumni and social/organizational psychologists. In essence this means that contributions from both disciplines do not reach beyond common sense supported by analytical tools. Particularly for the applied social psychologist this is a missed opportunity, as there is a wealth of theoretical/empirical material available through the average textbook. It just needs to be applied. This book sets out a methodology and discipline on *how* to do this.

When students learn to see the usefulness of the textbook materials and apply them systematically, this will not only improve the craft of the applied psychologist and make for happier clients, it will also contribute immensely to the relevance of the text and the motivation and satisfaction of the students.

Dr Peter Veen, 2007

HOW TO USE THIS TEXT

This is the first edition of *Applying Social Psychology*. The authors recognize the value of including certain learning tools to foster the experience of using a textbook for both students and teachers. Accordingly, the authors have decided to incorporate a range of features to illustrate the PATH method and make the book more user-friendly. Many of these features have arisen from feedback on courses in applied social psychology that we and others have taught over the years. We trust that these features will strike a chord with the readers and users of this text. The authors would like to thank Pieternel Dijkstra for help in preparing these features as well as for editorial assistance.

Key features in the textbook include the following:

1. Further readings
   If you want to find out more about the social psychological theories and research presented, we recommend a list of key readings in applied social psychology at the end of each chapter.
2. Assignments
   Each core chapter contains various assignments that enable students to practise applying social psychology to a diverse range of real-world problems. Each assignment focuses on a particular step in the PATH method. These assignments can be used by teachers to monitor and evaluate student progress or by the students themselves to monitor their own progress in the course.
3. Summaries
   At the end of each chapter a chapter summary is provided. These summarize the sequence of steps within that particular phase of the PATH method.
4. Figures and tables
   The text contains numerous tables and figures to support information in the text.
5. Updated research programmes
   This text contains a diversity of examples of key up-to-date research programmes in applied social psychology to illustrate the various aspects of the PATH method. We discuss research examples from around the world on a wide range of different social problems.
6. Text boxes
   The book contains several text boxes in which well-known social psychologists around the globe discuss why they got interested in applied social psychology and give examples of their applied research programmes.
7. Tests, measurements and instruments
   The text contains various examples of standard tests and measurement scales that are frequently used in applied social psychology. Examples are the self-esteem scale and the SYMLOG group observation instrument.

8. Glossary of key social psychological theories and concepts
   For best use of the text, we have identified a list of key social psychological theories and concepts and provide brief summaries of these in text boxes. It is advisable to use a core introductory text in social psychology for further details about theories and relevant research.
9. Case studies
   Each core chapter contains an example of research into a particular applied social psychology topic. This example serves as an illustration of how to conduct applied social psychology research.

INTRODUCTION AND BACKGROUND

Social psychology is not only a basic social science that studies the nature and determinants of human social behaviour. Social psychology is also an applied discipline of utmost relevance for all kinds of societal problems and issues. Social psychological theories and concepts are frequently used in a wide range of scientific disciplines such as environmental science, movement science, marketing, leisure science, business and management science, preventive medicine, social geography and gerontology, as well as in various subdisciplines of psychology such as clinical, environmental, health, industrial and organizational psychology.

Yet it seems that social psychologists themselves are not always aware of the practical value of their discipline. Most social psychological journals devote relatively little space to applied social psychology. Many traditional applied social psychology topics like aggression, conflict and cooperation in groups, leadership, obedience and helping have either completely disappeared from the literature or they are addressed in the literatures of other disciplines.

We are concerned about this development. Both of us have extensive experience with basic as well as applied social psychology research in a variety of social domains. Based on our own experiences, we believe that social psychology is uniquely placed to combine good theory-driven research with practical relevance. That is basically what Kurt Lewin, the founding father of modern social psychology, envisaged in the 1940s about the development of our discipline. It implies that social psychological processes should not just be studied in the lab, but also in a variety of field settings and with other populations than undergraduate students. It also implies that social psychologists should be interested in (and concerned about) how their findings might contribute to the solution of societal problems.

One major obstacle is that social problems often appear overwhelmingly complex and therefore it may not always be easy to see precisely how social psychology can contribute to their solution. Furthermore, all practical problems are unique in a way, and even if there is a lot of applied research in one specific area, these findings may not necessarily generalize to other domains.

This text presents a novel methodology for applying social psychology to practical social issues and developing an intervention programme. We refer to it as the PATH methodology. PATH is an acronym for the four essential steps in the model – **p**roblem, analysis, test (of model), and help. Each of the chapters in the book discusses one step of the PATH model.

We owe much to the pioneering work done by Peter Veen, who first published a text in the Dutch language in the 1980s with a new method for doing applied social psychology. Many generations of psychology students at Dutch universities were trained in the 'Method Veen'. To acknowledge this legacy, we have asked Veen to write the preface to this book. A completely new version of Veen's book was published in Dutch in 1995 by Abraham Buunk and Peter Veen. Although the present text is heavily inspired by these previous books, it is basically a new text and the first to appear in English with examples of applied social psychology research programmes from around the world.

We hope that our book will inspire many new generations of students across the world in doing social psychology and give them the necessary tools for applying social psychology to pressing social issues. There is much work to be done!

Abraham P. Buunk, Groningen, 2007
Mark Van Vugt, Canterbury, 2007

CHAPTER 1

APPLYING SOCIAL PSYCHOLOGY

Contents

Applying Social Psychology

EXAMPLE OF THE APPLICATION OF SOCIAL PSYCHOLOGICAL THEORIES

Can social psychology help in solving societal problems? And if this is the case, how can social psychology do so? Social psychology is a basic science which tries to build knowledge primarily through **experiments** and **surveys** (see for example Aronson, Wilson & Akert, 2002; Brehm, Kassin & Fein, 2005; Hewstone, Stroebe & Jonas, 2005; Hogg & Vaughan, 2005; Kenrick, Neuberg, & Cialdini, 2005; Myers, 2005).

Sometimes, the theories and findings from social psychology may seem a bit remote from the problems in society. However, many if not most societal problems have social psychological aspects (for example crime, racism, environmental pollution), and therefore social psychology may not only help in clarifying such problems, but also contribute to finding solutions. In this chapter we give an example of one such problem to illustrate this point, the debilitating problem of HIV/AIDS in Africa and the lack of support for HIV/AIDS victims. We also show how social psychological knowledge could lead to the development of a theoretical model on which an intervention might be based. Finally, we briefly outline the approach presented in this book, the PATH methodology, through which such models may be developed. This chapter thus summarizes the entire approach.

Step 1 – Problem: Formulating a Problem Definition

Whilst the increase in safe sex practices has meant the growth in the number of HIV infections has levelled off in the past decade, the number of people with AIDS has been rising all over the world. According to the World Health Organization in 2005 38.6 million people were infected with HIV globally, about 2.5 million more than in 2003. HIV/AIDS is especially a problem in Sub-Saharan Africa, where in 2005 around 26 million people were infected with HIV (WHO, 2005).

Although the possibilities for treatment have improved, HIV/AIDS still is an incurable disease that deeply affects the lives of those involved. In addition, more than any other disease, HIV/AIDS is surrounded by taboos and often leads to the stigmatization and isolation of patients (Dijker, Koomen & Kok, 1997). Patients are often abandoned by their families and friends. For adequate forms of medical and psychosocial help and support of people with HIV/AIDS in poor countries, considerably more money is required than is currently available. Yet while the treatment of people with HIV/AIDS has steadily improved, the willingness to donate money to help and support people with HIV/AIDS has decreased (Van Vugt, Snyder, Tyler & Biel, 2000).

Raising Money to Fight AIDS

A team of volunteers from a national HIV/AIDS charity foundation wishes to set up a campaign to raise funds for the purpose of providing medical and psychosocial care for people with HIV/AIDS in sub-Saharan Africa. Some team members argue that the campaign should not be too dramatic as it is now generally known how serious it is to be infected with HIV. They are concerned that showing too many depressing stories and pictures of people with HIV/AIDS will adversely affect the willingness to donate money. Others argue that just because there has been less media interest in HIV/AIDS recently, the campaign should highlight the severe and incurable nature of the disease. In doing so, there is a need to emphasize that the victims are not to blame, and that everybody is potentially at risk of contracting HIV. Accordingly, one part of the team wants to actively approach the media, whereas the others are concerned about the lack of media interest in this topic. A related point of debate concerns the campaign slogan. Should it be something positive, like 'Standing Up Against AIDS', or something more dramatic like 'Fighting the Horrors of AIDS'?

One volunteer suggests it would be better as part of the campaign to develop a product which people can buy, like a music CD of African artists, because in that case giving money would look less like charity. Another issue that comes up in the discussion is whether to use television and newspaper advertisements to raise money for the campaign, or to take a more personal, door-to-door, approach. Regarding the latter, should potential donors see a list of contributors and how much they have each contributed? One of the volunteers suggests showing just one large gift to encourage potential donors to match this donation. Other volunteers worry that this might put people off, because it will be difficult to match such an amount.

The Relevance of Social Psychology

The volunteer team decides to consult a social psychologist to help them develop their campaign. What suggestions should the social psychologist make? This psychologist might have little experience with campaigns to raise money for the fight against HIV/AIDS. Yet he will have conducted research on how to influence people and might know how to apply this to cases such as the HIV/AIDS campaign.

The social psychologist might of course conclude that more research is needed on why people donate money to charities. Given the urgency of the issue, however, this might take too long. Instead, there is an abundant amount of social psychological literature on people's willingness to donate money for charity that the psychologist can consult. Based on this, he might come up with specific suggestions on how to set up the campaign. Yet a better approach would be to first analyse the issue in greater detail and address the relevant causes and conditions for charity giving. Therefore, what he must do first is develop an adequate *problem definition*. This is the P-phase of the PATH methodology.

After a series of discussions with the team, the social psychologist defines the problem as follows:

> Many people in Africa suffer from HIV/AIDS, and there is insufficient funding to provide adequate forms of medical and psychosocial help and support for these people. Which factors determine potential donors' willingness to donate money for this cause? How can we set up a campaign that would raise money to help people with HIV/AIDS in Africa?

Step 2 – Analysis: Finding Explanations for the Problem

To identify what factors affect people's willingness to donate money for people with HIV/AIDS in Africa, the social psychologist formulates a broad set of questions that could be answered by the social psychological literature. There are two entries in the literature that immediately flash before him. The first is the literature on *helping*, **altruism**, *cooperation* and **prosocial behaviour** (see for example Batson & Powell, 2003; Van Vugt et al., 2000) which can tell him what motivates people to help others and give money for a good cause. The second is the literature on *social influence*, that can tell him what influence strategies are most effective in getting people to do what you want (see for example Prislin & Wood, 2005), in this case, donating money for people with HIV/AIDS in Africa.

The Altruism and Prosocial Literatures

The social psychologist decides to focus on the prosocial literature first, and formulates the problem in terms of two general questions:

1. When are people most inclined to help others?
2. What attributes of victims elicit the most helping responses?

He states these questions quite broadly because it is better at this stage to explore the literature more globally in order not to miss any relevant knowledge. Next, he conducts a search on the internet for books on helping with key words such as 'helping', 'altruism', 'cooperation', and 'prosocial behaviour', and finds a number of recent titles, including *The Altruism Question* by the American psychologist Dan Batson (1991), *The Psychology of Helping and Altruism* by the American social scientists David Schroeder, Jane Piliavin, Jack Dovidio, and Louis Penner (2006), the German social psychologist Hans Werner Bierhoff's *Prosocial Behaviour* (2002), and *Cooperation in Modern Society: Promoting the welfare of communities, states, and organizations* by the Dutch, American, and Swedish psychologists Mark Van Vugt, Mark Snyder, Tom Tyler and Anders Biel (2000). These books are all available in the local university library. After consulting the literature, the social psychologist concludes that there are, in fact, three different types of helping:

1. *Emergency intervention*, for example helping someone who is the victim of a robbery or accident.
2. *Organizational helping*, for example volunteering to take on an administrative job at the request of a manager.
3. *Sharing and donating resources*, for example donating money to a charity.

It is quite obvious that the present problem, raising money for people with HIV/AIDS, concerns the third prosocial behaviour. Yet, after reading the relevant literature, the social psychologist concludes that most of the prosocial literature deals with emergency helping and organizational helping. There is much less known about raising money for good causes. He explores the literature further, now by consulting PsychINFO – the electronic database that comprises all scientific articles and books in the field of psychology between 1872 and the present day. There he finds a theoretical model belonging to the Israeli social psychologist Shalom Schwartz, published in *Advances in Experimental Social Psychology* in 1977, which can be applied to all kinds of helping. The social psychologist decides to use Schwartz's model as a basis for understanding the problem that underlies the campaign, that is, how to increase people's willingness to donate money for people with HIV/AIDS in Africa. He presents this model to the team of volunteers and outlines the implications of the model for their campaign.

The Schwartz Model

In Schwartz's (1977) model there are various steps that affect people's prosocial behaviour. We present the most important here:

1. *Awareness*: There must be an awareness that others need help. The perceived need has to be prominent, clear and serious. We therefore need to draw attention to the fact that people with HIV/AIDS in many African countries face severe physical and mental distress, and need more medical, financial, and psychological support than is currently provided.
2. *Opportunities to help*: People must be aware that there are genuine opportunities for relieving the needs of people with HIV/AIDS. Therefore, the campaign must convey that there are various concrete actions that could improve the situation of victims.
3. *Ability to help*: People have to recognize their own *ability* to provide relief. If people feel helpless, their awareness of the problem is reduced, and they will not feel very motivated to offer help. Therefore it should be emphasized, for instance, that even small donations make a difference (for example, a one euro contribution means a family of five can eat for two days).
4. *Personal norms*: A major factor affecting helping behaviour is personal norms. These are feelings of moral obligation that one should help *specific needy others*. Emphasizing the needs of people with HIV/AIDS in Africa is an effective way to activate personal norms.
5. *Responsibility*: Finally, people also need to accept some *responsibility* for the problem in order to become involved and offer aid. As we will discuss later on, this is an obstacle in the case of the African HIV/AIDS problem.

Further, the literature suggests that people are more inclined to help when the recipients are considered blameless. In general, people with an illness evoke more sympathy if they are not held responsible for their fate (Graham, Weiner, Giuliano & Williams, 1993; Weiner, 1993). Also, the more sympathy individuals evoke the more help they receive (Rudolph et al., 2004). Knowing this, the social psychologist concludes that one of the primary aims of the campaign should be to eradicate the (erroneous) belief that people with HIV/AIDS in Africa are always themselves to blame for their illness.

Finally, helping is more likely when people are able to identify with the victims, for example, because they are similar in age, profession and **values**. Similarity leads to **empathy** – seeing oneself in someone else's place – which in turn leads to helping (Levy, Freitas, & Salovey, 2002; Stürmer et al., 2002; Batson, 1991). Although this may not be easy to achieve when the victims are in a remote place, this could nevertheless be accomplished by providing potential donors with *personal* reports from HIV/AIDS victims in Africa. This reduces the distance between helper and recipient and encourages people to empathize with victims.

Belief in a Just World

In the team meeting to discuss the campaign, someone suggests that people may respond differently to victims of disasters abroad rather than at home. The social psychologist tries to find out more about this possibility. He explores the literature further, and comes across a chapter in a German book that explicitly deals with this theme. This chapter – Solidarität mit der Dritten Welt [Solidarity with the Third World] – is written by the German psychologist Leon Montada. In this chapter Montada discusses the determinants of helping people in Third World countries, including giving to charity and political activities. From Montada's study it appears that helping is not related to empathy but to personal norms and one feeling a responsibility to do something. This sense of responsibility is caused by guilt about one's privileged situation, anger about the injustice/unfairness of the situation of people in poor countries, and the perception that people in poor countries are not responsible for their fate.

When the social psychologist reports this information to the team, the team decides to focus on the injustice that HIV/AIDS victims in the Third World receive and that due to the poverty and insufficient health care, help for people with HIV/AIDS is desperately needed. The issues of justice and fairness lead the psychologist to consider a **theory** – about the *belief in a* **just world** – formulated by the Canadian social psychologist Melvin Lerner (1980) which assumes that people have a natural tendency to believe they live in a just world in which everyone gets what they deserve. This belief is a common world view but while this belief is a universal phenomenon, there are presumably considerable differences between people as to the degree to which they share it. For someone who strongly adheres to the just world belief, events that shake this belief are threatening. People are especially upset by the unexplained suffering of others, for example, someone who has been working hard getting fired, or parents losing their child in an accident. For someone who strongly believes in a just world, such events are so upsetting that they will try to reduce this threat, sometimes by helping the victim to relieve their own suffering.

The social psychologist therefore concludes that the campaign would have to emphasize the unfairness of the plight of people with HIV/AIDS in Africa. Yet he also discovers that helping a victim is not the only way to deal with a threat to the just world belief. Lerner (1980) suggests that people also sometimes cognitively reinterpret an unjust event by holding victims responsible for their fate ('he could have used a condom') or derogating them ('he is morally irresponsible'). In addition, the social psychologist finds out about several studies which show that as individuals believe more strongly in a just world they are less likely to donate to charity goals in Third World countries (Campbell, Carr, & MacLachlan, 2001). Contrary to his initial thoughts he therefore concludes that the team should be careful to stress the injustice of the fate of people with HIV/AIDS in Africa.

Further scrutiny of the social psychological literature suggests a number of other factors that may influence **attitudes** towards people with HIV/AIDS in Africa. In general, people have more sympathy for victims the greater their belief a similar event might happen to them (Montada, 1992; Silver, Wortman & Crofton, 1990). More specifically, as individuals have more HIV/AIDS related experiences (such as knowing people who have HIV/AIDS) they are more willing to help people with HIV/AIDS (Cassel, 1995). Also, the greater the sympathy, the more social pressure there is to help the victims (Batson & Powell, 2003). On the basis of these and other findings, obtained in the social psychological literature, the social psychologist then builds a *process model,* an example of which is presented in Figure 1.1.

Step 3 – Test: Developing and Testing the Process Model

In the model, the key outcome variable is the willingness to donate money to help people with HIV/AIDS in Africa. There are a number of processes that influence this willingness, according to the model. One factor is the attitude towards people with HIV/AIDS. Based on the just world hypothesis, the more people believe that being infected with HIV is preventable, and the more they believe in a just world, the more they will hold people with HIV/AIDS responsible for their own fate and donate less. Thus, a potential problem for the campaign is that some people will feel that HIV/AIDS could be prevented by having safe sex, and that, as a result, many feel that people with HIV/AIDS somehow brought it upon themselves (For example, by living promiscuously).

Furthermore, research has shown that bad events happening to others evoke anger rather than compassion if they could have been prevented. More specifically, research shows that illnesses and diseases that are seen as controllable and preventable, such as AIDS and obesity, lead to a more negative attitude towards the patient and less helping than uncontrollable diseases, such as Alzheimer's (Weiner, Perry & Magnusson, 1988). This is especially the case among people who strongly believe in a just world (Mantler, 2001). As a consequence, people with HIV/AIDS are often negatively **stereotyped**, for instance, as having low moral worth (Walker et al., 1990). A social psychologist who has done significant work in the area of **prejudice** and **stereotyping** is Professor Susan Fiske of Princeton University (see Box 1.1).

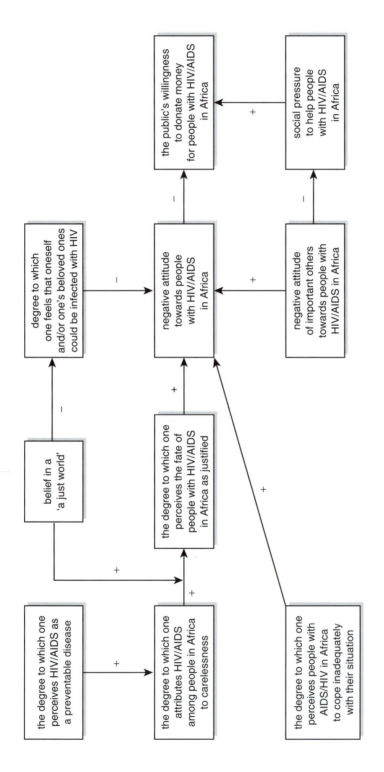

Figure 1.1 Process model: What determines the general public's willingness to donate money for people with HIV/AIDS in Africa?

Box 1.1   Interview with Professor Susan Fiske of Princeton University (USA)

'I always wanted to make the world a better place. My grandmother and great grandmother were suffragists (never suffragettes!). And my mother worked full-time as a civic volunteer for citizens' participation, urban neighbourhood organizations, cleaner air, and better parks. My father was a psychologist, so I put the two lines together, wanting to use psychology to improve things, especially for underdogs. But I realized, early on, that if you do not have the methodological tools to make a convincing scientific argument, no one will listen. My father was a methodologist, so that probably helped to drive that point home. Social psychology was the logical choice.

'What I love about social psychology is that it argues for the importance of the social situation, the impact of people on other people. If you think the important variance is in the situation (as opposed to, say, genes, or the first year of life), then to improve people's lives, you change the situation. This is an inherently progressive perspective.

'My most exciting professional impact was being cited by the Supreme Court. Ann Hopkins had been the star of her cohort at Price Waterhouse, billing more hours and respected by clients and colleagues alike. She was tough and exacting and effective. Unfortunately, she was also the only female partner candidate out of about 90 that year, and in a business utterly dominated by men at that point. People who didn't know her well, but who nevertheless voted, disliked this aggressive female manager. She was turned down for partner on the basis of allegedly deficient social skills, being advised that she could improve her chances by walking, talking, and dressing more femininely. Instead of going to charm school, she sued.

'Social psychology had a lot to offer Ann Hopkins, so I agreed to be an expert witness. I explained how perfectly well-intentioned PW partners could end up prescribing make-up and hair styling to a top-earning manager. **Gender roles** are intrinsically prescriptive, and this makes sexism ambivalent. Let me explain. People love the stereotypic homemaker but would not want her to run a company. At the same time, people respect the stereotypic businesswoman, but they tend to dislike her. Peter Glick and I captured this Catch-22 in our Ambivalent Sexism Inventory, which picks up on the benevolence toward traditional women and the hostility toward nontraditional women. Hostile sexism is not a new idea, but subjectively benevolent sexism is. And it goes a long way toward explaining certain kinds of barriers to women in the workplace.'

Interested in Susan Fiske's work? Then read, for instance:

(Continued)

KT

Fiske, S. T., Cuddy, A. J., Glick, P. & Xu, J. (2002). A model of (often mixed) stereotype content: Competence and warmth respectively follow from perceived status and competition. *Journal of Personality and Social Psychology, 82*, 878–902.
Fiske, S. T. & Taylor, S. E. (in press). *Social cognition: From brains to culture* (3rd edn). New York: McGraw-Hill.
Glick, P. & Fiske, S. T. (2001). An ambivalent alliance: Hostile and benevolent sexism as complementary justifications of gender inequality. *American Psychologist, 56*, 109–118.

A negative attitude towards people with HIV/AIDS is bolstered if they are perceived as not coping well with the situation. Research has shown victims who do not complain, and try to make the best of their situation, receive more help and sympathy (Dovidio, Piliavin, Schroeder & Penner, 2006). This implies that the campaign should not present people with HIV/AIDS in Africa as passive victims who do not try to improve their situation. Although the attitude towards people with HIV/AIDS in Africa will also be influenced by a perception of emotional closeness, this might be difficult to evoke, and therefore the social psychologist decides to leave this factor out of the model.

As we have seen, any willingness to help people with HIV/AIDS in Africa is also affected by feelings of moral obligation (Schwartz, 1977). Two factors, in particular, activate feelings of moral obligation. First, the perceived needs of those people with HIV/AIDS in Africa. A second factor is the perceived injustice of the poverty in Africa, but such feelings are weaker when people believe in a just world (Lerner, 1980). A willingness to donate money will, in addition to feelings of moral obligation and the attitude towards people with HIV/AIDS in Africa, also be affected by social pressure from relevant others and by the perceived effectiveness of helping (Batson, 1990; Van Vugt et al., 2000). The latter implies that the campaign must convince the public that the donated money is going to be spent wisely.

Research

The social psychologist could further suggest to the campaign team that some relationships in the process model are not yet clear in the literature and require further testing through research. For example, people might be willing to donate money out of sympathy with the victims, but also because of feelings of guilt (Cialdini & Trost, 1998; Huhmann & Brotherton, 1997). Therefore, what would be the result if the campaign were focused on the role of the West in causing poverty-related problems in sub-Saharan Africa, which would elicit guilt among potential donors? One consequence might be that people would feel personally responsible and give more to relieve their guilt. Another likely effect might be that this suggestion would infuriate people and that, out of dissent, they would contribute nothing. The social psychologist therefore decides that it would be wise to conduct some further research on the relationship between guilt and helping, before incorporating these ideas into the model.

Step 4 – Help: Towards an Intervention Programme

On the basis of the social psychologist's model, the team of volunteers decides that a number of factors, such as the belief in a just world, are difficult to change, but that a number of factors that may increase helping behaviour can possibly be influenced by a campaign. In particular, one aspect considered to be important is undermining people's tendency to devalue others with HIV/AIDS ('They have brought it upon themselves'). Another key point is that people are much keener to contribute money if they think their gift could 'make a difference' (Kerr, 1989; Oskamp, Burkharolt, Schultz, Hurin & Zelezny, 1998). It is thus worthwhile showing what even a small gift can do to relieve the problem. Further, more people will donate if they can do so easily and quickly and therefore donations over the internet should be made possible. Finally, too much negative information may cause people to devalue the victims or avoid paying attention to the campaign altogether, and, therefore, the message of the campaign will need to be decidedly positive.

After extensive discussion and an additional consultation of the social psychological literature, it is decided the campaign will have the following features:

1. Personal profiles of people with HIV/AIDS in Africa will be presented, who, despite their illness, are trying to make the best of their situation, but who clearly need medical and psychological help that is currently unavailable. Possible personal profiles could be:

   - a child who has been infected since birth and is now sick; without proper medication the child will die within a few months;
   - a woman who has been infected because she was raped; out of shame for the rape, her husband had left both her and their five children.

2. The tendency to blame people with HIV/AIDS in Africa will be tackled by the above examples, namely the fate of children born with HIV/AIDS and women who have suffered rape. Also to be emphasized is that due to poor information, poverty, and a lack of availability of contraceptives, people with HIV/AIDS in Africa are often unaware of the risks of unsafe sex and ways to prevent infection and therefore cannot be held personally accountable for contracting the disease.

3. Feelings of moral obligation will be induced by both showing that people with HIV/AIDS in Africa are in desperate need of help and also by making a subtle appeal to feelings of injustice with respect to the poverty in Africa.

4. The messages will be predominantly positive to prevent a negative attitude towards people with HIV/AIDS in Africa ('With a little gift, this person may have a long and productive life ahead of them').

5. It will be made clear that every gift no matter how small will help (for example, feeding a family for two days for as little as one euro), and it will be clearly stated for what purpose the donations will be used.

6. To lower the threshold to donate money, people will be able to donate money over the internet.

OTHER RELEVANT DECISIONS

Using the PATH methodology as a helpful tool, we have introduced you to the main steps in moving from a problem (how to raise money for people with HIV/AIDS in Africa) to the development of an intervention programme to tackle this same problem. We have formulated the details of a campaign to raise money for this worthy cause. Although the general approach of the campaign has now been formulated by the team with the help of an applied social psychologist, many more decisions still need to be made.

First, a decision must be made regarding the communication channel (McGuire, 1985). For example, the team will have to decide whether to run a media campaign (television, radio, internet), a door-to-door campaign, or a combination of the two. Each has its own logistical problems. The media will not easily provide broadcast time for free, especially if they consider the topic to be of insufficient interest to the public at large. For a door-to-door campaign one needs to recruit, organize and coordinate a large group of reliable volunteers throughout the country, which might be cumbersome.

Another issue is whether donors receive something in exchange for their gift, for example, a music CD by African artists for every donation over 50 euros. The helping literature suggests that this may be a good thing to do. The norm of reciprocity states that individuals feel best when they receive something in return for what they give (Buunk & Schaufeli, 1999; Cialdini & Trost, 1998). As a consequence, and considering the tendency to blame the victims, people might be more willing to give if they know they will receive something in return. Gifts are more likely associated with an acute disaster such as a drought or Tsunami. With the HIV/AIDS problem – a situation of prolonged suffering – people might be more willing to donate if they are to get something in return which will have intrinsic value to them, while at the same time they are doing something good. People can engage in such a transaction without having to take a position about the causes of the problem. They may think they are just getting a good deal.

Many other details will have to be decided, for example which product to offer, which media channels to use, and a slogan for the campaign. For many of these questions, there is relevant social psychological literature that could be consulted, for example, on persuasion (O'Keefe, 1990), communication (McGuire, 1985) and social influence (Schultz and Oskamp, 2000). In addition, there is an applied literature on how to set up fundraising campaigns (Clarke, Botting & Norton, 2001).

APPLYING SOCIAL PSYCHOLOGY: THE PATH FROM PROBLEM TO INTERVENTION

We believe that the PATH method helps social scientists to develop a theoretically-based intervention programme relatively quickly and smoothly. There is no denying that there are sometimes important obstacles in the way. For instance, it may take some time to formulate the problem, and some deliberation to focus on the most pressing elements of the problem. The problem may seem so complex that one cannot see 'the wood for the trees'. In addition, gathering the relevant social psychological literature might take time (although the internet has clearly facilitated the search process). There may be little relevant research on the topic or alternatively, there may be too many relevant social psychological theories and it will prove difficult to choose between them. Finally, it is difficult to tell whether or not an intervention is going to be successful. Even if interventions have been successful in the past, there is no guarantee one will work this time.

The PATH method offers a simple, systematic, step-by-step, easy-to-use methodology for applying social psychological theories to tackle a diversity of social issues. In sum, we can identify four essential steps in this methodology:

1. PROBLEM – from the problem to a problem definition; identifying and defining the problem;
2. ANALYSIS – from a problem definition to analysis and explanation; formulating appropriate concepts and developing theory-based explanations;
3. TEST – from explanations to a process model; developing and testing an explanatory process model;
4. HELP – from a process model to interventions; developing and evaluating a programme of interventions.

We briefly describe below each of these four steps of the PATH method. In each of the chapters that follow, these steps will be outlined in greater detail and with plenty of illustrative examples.

Step 1 – Problem: From the Problem to a Problem Definition

Arriving at an adequate problem definition requires much consideration and deliberation. Usually, the problem definition is more extensive than the one we formulated earlier in this chapter where the team knew already that they wanted to set up a fundraising campaign to help people with HIV/AIDS in Africa. Often there is just a general feeling within a team, community, or organization that there is a problem and something must be done without much further thought being involved. In the example of an HIV/AIDS fundraising campaign, the team of volunteers may have simply been frustrated about a lack of attention towards the plight of people with HIV/AIDS in Africa within their country. Getting this attention would require quite a different approach than that required in setting up a fundraising campaign. Further, an internal controversy on policy priorities within a charity organization is often better dealt with by organizational psychologists and consultants.

As will be addressed in Chapter 2, it is very important to describe precisely *what* the problem is (for example, 'How can we raise money to help people with AIDS in Africa?'). But even when the problem is presented clearly, other questions also need to be asked. We must assess if the problem is sufficiently concrete rather than it being a general scientific question like: 'How can we make people more altruistic?' Also, *why* is it a problem at all (for example, 'People with HIV/AIDS in Africa suffer greatly and have few opportunities for treatment') and for *whom* it is a problem (for example, 'people with HIV/AIDS in Africa, their families, and their countries')? In addition, we must specify the main *causes* of the problem, in this case why we think people might be reluctant to give money to this particular charitable cause, for example because they find it difficult to empathize with people in Africa or there is competition coming from other charity organizations. Further, we should specify the population we aim to target with our intervention (*target group*). Who do we need to convince that this problem has to be solved? Who must help solve this problem? In the example of an HIV/AIDS fundraising campaign, the volunteer team should determine who they want to encourage to donate money; the general public or specific subgroups (such as families with high incomes), private persons or organizations and companies? Because they want to convince as many people as possible to donate money, the team in the above example chose to target the general public.

Finally, the *key aspects* of the problem need to be considered. That is, a good problem definition makes clear that the problem has an *applied* rather than a basic nature, and is formulated in *concrete* terms. In the example of an HIV/AIDS fundraising campaign, this would give answers to the question of why people may be reluctant to give money to HIV/AIDS charities. Last but not least, there must be a feeling that the problem has *social psychological* aspects and that it is potentially *solvable* or relievable.

In the first discussions with the AIDS team of volunteers, the focus might be on the irresponsible attitude of some political leaders in Africa with respect to HIV/AIDS, or the attitude of the Roman Catholic Church towards condom use. It is obvious that these issues are not problems that social psychologists can easily solve (or should even want to solve). Changing the attitudes of political and religious leaders may be done by using social psychological knowledge, but it probably requires a sustained political and diplomatic effort.

In contrast, changing the attitudes of the general public towards people with HIV/AIDS in Africa is a good example of the type of issue to which social psychologists may contribute. Such attitudes are social psychological constructs, and there is a wealth of theorizing and research on how such attitudes may be changed. In general, social psychological factors concern behaviours (for example, giving money), attitudes (say, a negative evaluation of people with HIV/AIDS), cognitions (for example, negative perceptions of people with HIV/AIDS), and affective/emotional responses (say, a fear of AIDS). When the problem cannot be defined along one or more of these terms – behaviours, attitudes, cognitions, affective responses – it is probably not suitable for a PATH analysis.

Step 2 – Analysis: From a Problem Definition to Analysis and Explanation

Once the problem has been defined in terms of one or more social psychological constructs, the second step is to come up with social psychological explanations for the problem. Before doing so, one first has to decide what the *outcome variable* is, that is, which variable eventually needs changing. In the example of an HIV/AIDS fundraising campaign, it is a willingness to donate money for people with HIV/AIDS in Africa. As will be described in Chapter 3, after having defined this variable, in the *divergent* stage, one starts looking for explanations through techniques such as 'free association' and through applying relevant social psychological theories. In the development of a process model to explain a willingness to donate money for people with HIV/AIDS in Africa, the psychologist in the example knew right away that he had to look in the literature on helping behaviour and prosocial behaviour. Through a search in the helping literature, he found the model by Schwartz (1977) that seemed quite relevant.

In retrospect it might seem evident to look into this literature, but someone without a background in social psychology might not have known where to look. Moreover, even when confining oneself to the social psychological literature on helping, one might have found many different models and theories. There are for example **social exchange** and reciprocity theories, emphasizing the role of egotistic concerns in helping (Buunk & Schaufeli, 1999; Hardy & Van Vugt, 2006). By performing acts of kindness individuals may receive many benefits. They may, for instance, feel happier (Lyubomirsky, Sheldon & Schkade, 2005), experience positive self-evaluations and a boost in self-esteem (for example, 'I did something good today!', 'I am a caring person'), receive praise, or experience the joy of seeing the needy person experience relief. In addition, helpers may avoid negative feelings, such as shame or guilt (Batson & Powell, 2003). There are also theories that emphasize truly altruistic motivations, for example, **empathy-altruism theory** (Batson, 1991; Bierhoff & Rohmann, 2004). The basic idea of this theory is that empathic concern motivates altruistic behaviour aimed at relieving a victim's suffering. This theory suggests, for example, that people will support HIV/AIDS victims in Africa if they can easily see themselves in their shoes (namely, high empathy). After generating many different explanations, one must then reduce the explanations based on their relevance, validity and plausibility. In the example of an HIV/AIDS fundraising campaign, the social psychologist disregards the empathy factor as people may not feel very similar to people with HIV/AIDS in Africa.

To determine the validity of the social psychological theories, it is important to assess the extent to which the typical experiments on which the theory is based represent the real world. Many theories in their abstract form may seem readily applicable in a given situation, but what people often tend to forget is that most theories in social psychology are usually based upon a specific research paradigm that may only be generalized to a limited number of situations in real life. This concern refers to the **external validity** of an experiment. It is possible that research findings, because of the specific research paradigm or limitations in samples or settings, can only be applied to a limited number of real-life situations. In that case the external validity of an experiment is low.

For example, in a typical example of the experiments that form the basis of Batson's (1991) empathy-altruism theory, people observe another person ('the worker') who they think is suffering from a series of uncomfortable electric shocks that have been administered to them by the experimenter for failing to give correct answers. They are given a chance to help the worker by taking the shocks themselves. There are at least two major differences between this situation and the situation of donating money to people with HIV/AIDS in Africa. First, it concerns others who are close in proximity, and, second, one is asked to take on the suffering of the victim oneself. Thus, Batson's theory may have limited relevance for this particular problem.

Step 3 – Test: From Explanations to a Process Model

On the basis of a limited set of variables resulting from the previous stage, a process model can be formulated like the one presented in Figure 1.1. (How to build such a model is described in much more detail in Chapter 4.) The model contains the outcome variable that must be influenced, in this case a willingness to donate money for people with HIV/AIDS. In addition, the model should primarily contain variables that can be influenced, at least to some extent, and should describe the relationship between the variables in the form of a process model. This process model is at the core of PATH methodology. Although the model in Figure 1.1 seems plausible, this is by no means the only model that could have been formulated on the basis of the selected variables. Why, for example, does the belief in a just world not directly affect a negative attitude towards people with HIV/AIDS in Africa? Why does the way in which people with HIV/AIDS in Africa cope with the situation not lead to feelings of moral obligation? Why is a willingness to donate money not directly affected by the perceived injustice of poverty in Africa?

In general, the process model specifies just a few possible relationships between its variables. Any given variable should not affect more than two or three other variables. This forces practitioners to be selective and specific about the causal relationships in the model. By including too many relationships, it may become a model in which 'everything is explained by everything', and it would be difficult to formulate specific interventions based on it.

In the example of an HIV/AIDS fundraising campaign, the social psychologist formulated his model on the basis of existing empirical research. However, often one is forced to formulate a model in which it is not yet clear to what extent the various paths between the variables are empirically supported. Ultimately, a model is only complete if there is sufficient evidence from research for the relationships between the variables. (In Chapter 4 we discuss how to assess the empirical support for the model.) Of course, because we aim to develop explanations and interventions based on social psychological knowledge, in the present approach we need to use as much existing knowledge as possible. This knowledge can be derived from basic social psychological research as well as from other research more or less directly applied to the problem (Fliszar & Clopton, 1995; Montada, 2001).

Frequently, however, one can only find empirical evidence that validates *parts* of the process model, and not the entire model. In the example of an HIV/AIDS fundraising campaign, there is, for instance, little research on willingness to donate money for people with HIV/AIDS in Africa, or on charity donation in general. If one cannot find research on the specific problem (for example, charity donation) to support (parts of) the model, one may look for evidence in research on the generic behaviour (for example, altruism). The social psychologist that advised the volunteer team, for instance, found support for (parts of) his model in the general literature on helping.

Step 4 – Help: From a Process Model to Intervention

The final and often most difficult step is to move from the process model to a help or intervention programme. (This is described in Chapter 5.) To be able to develop an intervention programme, it is important that the model contains primarily factors that can be influenced through intervention. Most social psychological variables, such as attitudes and **social norms,** can be targeted by interventions, but factors such as gender, personality or other deeply rooted **traits** and values cannot (at least not by a social psychologist). Of course, it might seem obvious to include gender or personality in the model, because for instance women have more empathy or are more agreeable, and thus are more inclined to donate money. However, although such factors may be very important, it is difficult to build an intervention programme around them. Even factors that may seem less deeply rooted in human nature, such as prejudice towards gay people, may be difficult to change, especially via media campaigns.

The step from the Test to the Help phase is huge. The social psychologist must first come up with as many interventions as possible, aimed at the most promising and important factors in the model. Often this intervention will contain behavioural training, a programme of education, information, rules or prescriptions. Shaping the programme in such detail that it can be implemented usually takes a lot of time, energy, and creativity.

PROBLEMS WITH APPLYING THEORIES

It is not easy to apply social psychological theories to social problems. Most general knowledge in social psychology is derived from laboratory experiments (see any social psychology text), and these have several important limitations (Aronson, Wilson & Akert, 2002). We will now discuss three of the most important limitations of this type of research: oversimplification, external validity, and contradictory evidence.

Oversimplification

The situation examined in experiments is virtually, by definition, a reduction and simplification of reality. A single laboratory experiment can never examine the complex interplay of variables that affect human social behaviour in the real world and can examine at most two or three factors. For example, the social psychologist assisting the AIDS team concluded from laboratory research on emergency helping (Latané & Darley, 1970) that often **bystanders** do not intervene when they see another person is in need. One could come up with numerous factors that may affect a willingness to help in such situations, including the bystander's **personality**, family background, **mood**, preoccupation with other issues, fear, embarrassment, lack of control, and the age and sex of the victim. Yet in the classic 'bystander experiment' Latané and Darley (1970) only examined one factor, that is, the number of other people present. They showed that a willingness to help someone allegedly experiencing a seizure was reduced the more other people were present. Although Latané and Darley's experiment is a very interesting one, it did not show how important this factor was in comparison with other factors that may influence willingness to help, such as the victim's age or sex, or how it interacted with other factors.

Another example of the limitation of laboratory experiments is a research programme by the American social psychologist Donn Byrne (1971) on the effect of attitude similarity on attraction. In a typical similarity experiment participants fill out an attitude questionnaire. They are then presented with a second questionnaire that has allegedly been completed by another participant. However, the experimenter has fabricated this questionnaire in such a way that it has either 25 per cent or 75 per cent of the attitudes in common with the participant's attitudes. In general, it appears that the more attitudes one has in common with the other person, the more one likes the other individual, and this is a quite strong effect. However, in real life, such as when a dating agency wants to match people, other factors such as physical attractiveness, status, or educational level may be more important than attitude similarity. It is, of course, possible to examine such factors as these in experiments. For example, Byrne, Ervin and Lamberth (1970) showed that attitude similarity and physical attractiveness determined to a similar degree the attraction to someone of the opposite sex. Although researchers can include a second, third or even fourth variable in their experiments, it is impossible to include all potentially relevant factors in a laboratory experiment. The social psychologist must assess what the most important variables are, for example, through a survey among the target population.

External Validity

A second limitation is that all kinds of factors in real life may obscure the impact of the variables that are so clearly manipulated in experiments. For instance, in the experiments by Byrne (1971), participants knew exactly the real attitudes of the other person. In real life one seldom knows how other people think about certain issues. Several studies on the relation between attitude similarity and attraction show that, unlike what Byrne's experiments suggest, *actual* attitude similarity scarcely affects initial feelings of attraction. What really counts is one's *perception* of attitude similarity, that is, the degree to which individuals *believe* another person to have similar attitudes. This determines attraction, not the degree to which attitudes actually *are* similar. Buunk and Bosman (1986), for instance, found that whereas spouses showed a low degree of actual attitude similarity, they showed a high degree of perceived attitude similarity (for a review, see Sunnafrank, 1992). Thus, if one had been asked by an organization how to make cohesive teams, and one had proposed to form teams on the basis of the actual attitude similarity among the members, the results would have been quite disappointing.

KT Another example of this limitation comes from research on unconscious **priming**. There is considerable evidence that priming individuals with stimuli that are offered subliminally, that is without being consciously perceived, may affect behaviour. In a study by the American social psychologist John Bargh and his colleagues (Bargh, Chen & Burrows, 1996), participants were primed on politeness or rudeness through a so-called scrambled sentence task. When they were primed on politeness, participants in a later, unrelated situation, interrupted the experimenter who was talking with someone else less often than participants primed on rudeness. Despite the striking results of such experiments, in real life the success of these interventions may be weak or there may be ethical concerns.

Contradictory Evidence

Another limitation of social psychological research is that studies often produce contradictory findings. For instance, Griffith (1970) found that participants who waited in a room with uncomfortable environmental conditions (high temperature, high humidity level) liked the person with whom they were waiting less than participants who waited in a room with comfortable environmental conditions (normal temperature and low humidity level). Yet Bell and Baron (1974) failed to replicate this effect. Other social psychological research shows that people tend to like others *more* when they meet them in fear-arousing, uncomfortable situations (Dutton & Aron, 1974).

Findings like these may be confusing and difficult to interpret. Fortunately, researchers are sometimes able to reconcile contrasting findings. Often, contradictory results stem from the fact that on numerous occasions studies have subtly different methods. Kenrick and Johnson (1979) found, for instance, that negative feelings which are due to uncomfortable circumstances will induce aversion for another person, a stranger, even when those being studied do not interact with this person. In contrast, when individuals actually interact with someone uncomfortable circumstances can often *increase* liking. This illustrates that one should not take the conclusions from experiments as general truths, but that one should carefully examine the experimental paradigm on which a particular finding is based before applying it to the real world.

From a broader perspective, seemingly contradictory conclusions from experiments support the idea that humans are complex social beings with many different behavioural tendencies. For example, they will seek out factual confirmation of who they are as well as flattering information on how good they are; they are egoistical as well as altruistic; they are rational as well as emotional. There are numerous theories in social psychology, and each theory tends to emphasize a distinct human tendency. For instance, Batson's (1991) empathy-altruism theory emphasizes that people have a basic tendency to respond with altruistic empathy to others, whereas social exchange theory emphasizes that people first and foremost pursue their self-interest in helping relations (Thibaut & Kelley, 1959). Swann's self-confirmation theory (see, for example, Swann, Stein-Seroussi & Giesler, 1992) suggests that people tend to seek out information that confirms their self-image, be it positive or negative, whereas **self-esteem** theory (Baumeister & Tice, 1990) would suggest that people simply prefer all information to make them feel good about themselves.

CONCLUSION

This book introduces the PATH model, a step-by-step approach for addressing and resolving societal problems through the application of social psychological theory and knowledge, from the formulation of the problem to the shaping of interventions. Although every practitioner can potentially benefit from PATH methodology, some background in social psychological theory is desirable.

The PATH model should not be used in a rigid way. Going from a problem to intervention is usually an iterative process, and one frequently moves back and forth between the different steps in the model. For instance, one may start with defining the problem, but when exploring the literature, one can discover that there are certain aspects of the problem that one has overlooked. In that case, one first has to redefine the problem. Or one may see explanations and solutions before having formulated a clear problem definition. There is nothing wrong with adapting the problem definition after having explored the research literature. It is even advisable to do so. What counts is not strictly following the steps of the PATH model, but developing a clear problem definition, a process model that fits the empirical findings as closely as possible, and an effective intervention.

SUGGESTED FURTHER READING

Dovidio, J. F., Piliavin, J. A., Schroeder, D. A. & Penner, L. A. (2006). *The social psychology of pro-social behaviour*. Mahwah, NJ: Erlbaum.

Omoto, A. & Snyder, M. (1995). Sustained helping without obligation: motivation, longevity of service, and perceived attitude. *Journal of Personality and Social Psychology, 68*, 671–686.

Schultz, P. W. & Oskamp, S. (2000). *Social psychology: An applied perspective*. Upper Saddle River, NJ: Prentice-Hall

Van Vugt, M., Snyder, M., Tyler, T. & Biel, A. (2000). *Cooperation in modern society: Promoting the welfare of communities, states, and organisations*, p. 245. London: Routledge.

KT

Box 1.2 A case study: *Social comparison* in adjustment to breast cancer

KT

Patients who have a serious illness, such as cancer, often feel fearful and uncertain about their future and worry that they are coping poorly or losing their grip on reality. This type of **stress** may lead to a longer recovery period and increase both the emotional as well as the financial burden of the disease. Helping patients to cope optimally with their disease is therefore an issue of great concern.

Patients often cope with their illness by comparing themselves with other patients, namely by making so-called social comparisons (Festinger, 1954). Social comparisons may contribute to adjustment through two functions. First, by comparing themselves to others in the same situation, patients may learn to what extent their reactions are reasonable and normal (*self-evaluation*). Second, serious illness can pose a great threat to patients' self-esteem since it often brings a great deal of changes that are critical to their identity (for instance, with regard to body image, occupation, valued activities, and close relationships). By comparing themselves to other patients, they may restore and enhance their self-esteem (for

KT

example, 'It could have been much worse'; **self-enhancement**).

To make accurate self-evaluations patients may best compare themselves with similar others, namely patients who are about equally ill, because these patients provide the most useful information about how to cope. In contrast, when individuals are motivated to enhance their self-esteem, they are best served by comparisons with patients who are either worse (*downward comparisons*) or better off (*upward comparisons*).

The question that arises is whether patients benefit more from social comparisons through self-evaluations or self-enhancement. In others words, in adjusting to their illness, with whom do patients prefer to compare themselves: with similar others, or with patients who are better or worse off? To answer this question the American psychologists Joanne Wood, Shelley Taylor and Rosemary Lichtman* interviewed 78 breast cancer patients about their illness and the ways they coped, including the type of social comparisons they made. These researchers found that over 60 per cent of respondents said that another patient was coping less well than she was; 80 per cent said that they adjusted at least somewhat better than other women. In other words, the researchers found a preponderance of downward comparison, indicating that, among breast cancer patients, self-enhancement is the most dominant motive for social comparison.

Findings like these are important for interventions that aim to help patients adjust (see Buunk, Gibbons & Visser, 2002). Consistent with patients' preference for downward comparisons, they may, for instance, point out what patients are still able to do (rather than what they cannot do any more).

* Wood, J.V., Taylor, S.E. & Lichtman, R.R. (1985). Social comparison in adjustment to breast cancer. *Journal of Personality and Social Psychology, 49*, 1169–1183.

ASSIGNMENT 1

Read Box 1.2 (pp. 22–3) Imagine you are asked to develop an intervention programme to enhance the well-being of cancer patients on the basis of the study described in this box (Wood, Taylor & Lichtman, 1985).

(a) Describe in this context:

- *what* exactly the problem is that you aim to solve with the intervention programme;
- *why* the problem is a problem (in, among others, emotional, financial and societal terms) and since *when*;
- for *whom* it is a problem (for patients or also, for instance, for their relatives and/or for taxpayers);
- what are the possible *causes* of the problem (for instance, relevant behaviours, emotions or cognitions, lack of information);
- *whom* you aim to target with your intervention (target group);
- the key *aspects* of the problem (applied, concrete, social psychological, is the problem solvable or relievable).

(b) Discuss to what extent the belief in a just world, as described in this chapter, may influence cancer patients' well-being when they socially compare themselves with other patients. To what extent do you think that the belief in a just world is relevant to the intervention programme?

(c) Design an intervention on the basis of the results of Wood, Taylor and Lichtman's study (see Box 1.2) to relieve the problem you have described in (a) above. Describe specifically the social psychological variables you aim to manipulate by intervention and by what means you aim to do so and why.
You may read the following articles to come up with ideas about interventions for cancer patients:

Bennenbroek, F.T.C., Buunk, B.P., Stiegelis, H.E., Hagedoorn, M., Sanderman, R., Van den Bergh, A.C.M. & Botke, G. (2003). Audiotaped social comparison information for cancer patients undergoing radiotherapy: Differential effects of procedural, emotional and coping information. *Psycho-Oncology, 12(6)*, 567–579.

Bennenbroek, F.T.C., Buunk, B.P., Van der Zee, K.I. & Grol, B. (2002). Social comparison and patient information: What do cancer patients want? *Patient Education and Counselling, 47(1)*, 5–12.

Stiegelis, H.E., Hagedoorn, M., Sanderman, R., Buunk, B.P., Van den Bergh, A.C.M., Botke, G. & Ranchor, A.V. (2004). The impact of an informational self-management intervention on the association between control and illness uncertainty before and psychological distress after radiotherapy. *Psycho-Oncology, 12(6)*, 567–579.

CHAPTER 2

THE PROBLEM PHASE:
FROM A PROBLEM TO
A PROBLEM DEFINITION

Contents

The Problem Phase: From a Problem to a Problem Definition

INTRODUCTION

Social problems are everywhere around us. Open up a newspaper, watch television or listen to the radio, and suddenly you are confronted with a rich variety of social issues, many of which have a social psychological dimension. Regardless of whether it concerns the problem of teenage pregnancies, smoking and health, divorce, anti-social behaviour in residential communities, school truancies, prejudice towards ethnic minority members or even global warming, social psychological factors play a role in all of them. Indeed, as societies grow larger and individuals live and work more closely together, social and environmental problems are bound to rise, affecting an ever larger proportion of the population (Gardner & Stern, 1996; Van Vugt et al., 2000). Hence, there is an urgent need for the involvement of social psychologists to study these problems, and to offer solutions while working together with fellow scientists and policy makers (see, for example, Aronson, Wilson & Akert, 2002; Brehm, Kassin & Fein, 2005; Hewstone, Stroebe & Jonas, 2005; Hogg & Vaughan, 2005; Kenrick, Neuberg & Cialdini, 2005; Myers, 2005). This is not to say, of course, that all or most societal problems can be directly attributed to social psychological factors.

For example, the primary cause of lung cancer is smoking, and pollution is primarily caused by the use of cars. Hardly social psychological matters, so it seems. Yet social psychologists will try to understand why, despite the widespread knowledge about the health risks, so many individuals still continue to smoke (Gibbons, Gerrard & Lando, 1991; Stroebe & Stroebe, 1995). Or they will investigate why most people continue to drive cars, although there are sometimes much better travel options available (Joireman, Van Lange & Van Vugt 2004; Van Vugt, Meertens & Van Lange, 1995).

Perhaps the clearest illustration of the important role for social psychology can be seen from a sample of headlines that appeared in British newspapers in the week that this chapter was being written. This list reads as follows:

1. Treeplanting schemes may help to reduce carbon emissions.
2. Sale of the 'morning-after' pill on the increase.
3. Government to build a network of health care walk-in centres near companies.
4. Workplace bullying on the increase with nearly 80 per cent of human resources departments saying it exists in their firm, according to a new survey.
5. One in seven UK students drops out of university.

6. Efforts to promote 'lifelong learning' using computers have done little to increase the number of adults in education.
7. Threatening or abusive youngsters targeted as part of a new crackdown on anti-social behaviour.
8. Police use of anti-terror laws leading to arrests of the wrong people, according to think tank's study.
9. Nottingham charity says fewer people are willing to get involved because of commitments in modern life.
10. Police are looking for more ethnic police officers to join the force.

This summary shows not just that our society (as well as many societies around the world) is facing a diversity of problems today, it also indicates that there are vast differences in the way these problems are stated. Some of them are based merely on an observation (for example, one in seven students drops out of university) and it is not always that clear what the problem is exactly (the *what* question). Others are based on a piece of systematic research (for example, workplace bullying is on the increase), and while it is immediately clear what the problem is, it does not state anything about why it is perceived as a problem or when it first appeared (the *why* question). Other statements do give a potential cause for the problem (for example, a charity saying fewer people get involved because of **commitments** in modern life) – the *causes* question – but it is unclear for whom it is a problem, how widespread this problem is (the *for whom* question) and whose cooperation is essential to solve the problem (the question about the *target group*). Finally, there are problems which are merely expressed as an intention to do something about an unsatisfying situation (for example, the police force looking for more ethnic officers), but it is unclear how these can be solved (the *aspects* question). Thus, although from each of these above statements inferences can be made about what the problem is, important details are lacking, and many more questions need to be asked in order to establish a formal problem definition.

Towards a Problem Definition

What do we mean by a problem description? By this we mean a clear and precise description of *what* the problem is, *why* and for *whom* it is believed to be a problem. Also we should identify the *target group* for intervention in the problem definition. In addition, a problem definition should give some insight into some possible *causes* and *key aspects* of the problem, such as whether this particular problem is an *applied, concrete* and *social psychological* problem, and whether the problem is *solvable* or relievable.

In articles appearing in social psychological journals, little attention is usually given to the process of formulating a problem definition. This is perhaps more understandable in the case of basic social psychological research, in which researchers are primarily interested in understanding the mechanisms underlying a particular social problem. For example, in their **empathy-altruism research**, Batson and his colleagues are primarily (but not exclusively) interested in understanding the conditions under which individuals are motivated to help others in need (Batson, 1991; Batson & Powell, 2003). They are less concerned with applying their knowledge to promote altruistic behaviour in society and leave it to applied psychologists to use their insights for developing intervention.

Yet even in articles with a more applied focus, a systematic problem analysis is often lacking. As an illustration, research articles on environmentally sustainable behaviours, such as household recycling, household energy use or carpooling, often begin by stating that there is a problem (the depletion of environmental resources) and then quickly move into the particular behaviour under investigation (for examples from our own work, see Van Vugt, 2001; Van Vugt et al., 1995). However, a more systematic problem analysis would reveal that domestic energy use, for example, represents only a third of total energy consumption in a country (Gardner & Stern, 1996). Thus, from an intervention point of view, it would make more sense to concentrate on energy savings from bulk consumers, such as businesses and factories.

An elegant example of research based on a problem definition is work on volunteering by Mark Snyder (see Box 2.1), Allen Omoto and colleagues (Kiviniemi, Snyder & Omoto, 2002; Omoto & Snyder, 1995; Omoto, Snyder & Martino, 2000). In their research they first recognized, through surveys and interviews, that the act of volunteering – to assist people with HIV/AIDS – served different psychological functions for different volunteers. Some volunteers were primarily driven by a pan-altruistic motivation to help others, while others were motivated more by a specific attachment to the community of people with HIV/AIDS or by the effects of volunteering for their personal growth and development. On the basis of these results, they argued that it would be wise to develop a volunteer recruitment campaign that would target individuals on the basis of their main motive for volunteering. They were indeed more successful in their recruitment if they tailored their message to a specific target audience of potential volunteers (Kiviniemi, Snyder & Omoto, 2002). Below is an interview with Professor Mark Snyder, from the University of Minnesota, about his applied social psychological research.

Box 2.1 Interview with Professor Mark Snyder of the University of Minnesota (USA)

'As a psychologist, I wear many hats. I am a basic scientist, and I am an applied researcher. I work in the laboratory, and I work in the field. I address problems of theoretical significance, and ones of practical concern. Rather than keeping these various facets of my professional identity separate from each other, I have worked to integrate them. Thus, I have a particular fondness for research that, at one and the same time, advances the state of theoretical understanding and also speaks to the challenges that confront society.

'Accompanying my belief that social science should contribute to solving the problems of society has been a longstanding fascination with people who themselves take action for the benefit of society. In my research, I have sought to understand how and why people become actively involved in doing good for others and for society. Such involvement can take the form of participation in volunteerism and philanthropy, community and neighbourhood organizations, social activism and political movements. In this research on social action, my collaborators and I are discovering why individuals become involved in various forms of social action, what sustains their involvement over time, and the consequences of such action for individuals and for society.

'A defining feature of my work is its focus on real people involved in real social action in real settings. For instance, in our studies of volunteerism, we have followed volunteers over the entire course of their service with community-based organizations, thereby allowing us to chart their life histories as volunteers and to study the unfolding processes of volunteerism. Such work can be time-consuming and effortful but has been well worth it. For such research is contributing meaningfully, I believe, to an emerging understanding of the nature of volunteerism and other forms of social action. Moreover, it is speaking directly, I believe, to critical concerns with the role of individual and collective involvement in society. And, for me, it is extremely rewarding to be engaged in scientific activity in ways that can deliver benefits to science and to society – a 'win-win' situation for all concerned, I believe.'

Interested in Mark Snyder's work? Then read, for instance:

Snyder, M., Omoto, A.M. & Lindsay, J. (2004). Sacrificing time and effort for the good of others: The benefits and costs of volunteerism. In A.G. Miller (Ed.), *The social psychology of good and evil* (pp. 444–468). New York: Guilford Press.

Stürmer, S., Snyder, M. & Omoto, A.M. (2005). Prosocial emotions and helping: The moderating role of group membership. *Journal of Personality and Social Psychology, 88(3)*, 532–546.

Reformulating the Problem

From the above discussion, it should be clear that many of the problems stated in our 'news item' list should be rephrased and reformulated in order to reach a more formalized problem definition. First, many of these problems were stated in such generic terms that it is unclear what the problem was (for example, in the case of the drop outs among UK students) or how it could be tackled (for example, the police force wanting more ethnic police officers). When it is stated that the sale of the morning-after pill is on the increase, does this imply that there is actually a problem with the preventative use of contraceptives (condoms, birth control pills)? Furthermore, if there is a problem with contraceptive use, how many men and women in the UK (or in the whole of Europe or the world) are affected by it? Finally, it does not tell us anything about where the problem lies. For instance, do people forget to take contraceptives or are they not readily available to them? In sum, such global statements must be made more concrete in order to be useful for further investigation.

Second, a more detailed problem analysis could reveal that the real problem is different from the one that is stated. For example, a lack of volunteers for the Nottingham charity may have nothing to do with people having other time commitments. It may, for instance, have more to do with dissatisfaction among current and potential volunteers about the activities of this specific charity. A systematic problem analysis could even reveal that there is no problem at all. If after further scrutiny it appears that the 'one in seven UK students' that drop out from university finds a useful and rewarding alternative career path (for example, as plumbers), there may be little reason for further investigation.

Third, even if it is totally clear what the problem is then there is an array of different solutions that one could think of for solving it. Some of them may have nothing to do with psychology. Carbon emissions, for example, could be cut drastically if all cars were fitted with catalytic converters (giving clean engines; see Van Vugt et al., 1995). Ensuring this happens would involve legislation to force car companies to adopt this technology. There is little involvement by social psychologists in this kind of intervention (although a social psychologist could, for instance, assess the willingness of car companies to accept legislation).

Finally, if there is a clear social psychological dimension to the problem then it is a challenge for the social psychologist to find an appropriate theory or paradigm from a toolbox of different theories to investigate this further. For example, the problem of bullying in the workplace could be studied from a gender perspective (Quine, 2002) if it appears that women are predominantly the victims, either from a power framework perspective (if it appears that bosses bully subordinates) or from an intergroup perspective (if it appears that it mainly occurs between departments).

In a similar vein, the problem of absenteeism at work could be studied from a social exchange perspective (if it appears that people feel they put more effort into their work in comparison to what they receive in return), a social comparison perspective (if it appears that people feel frustrated and deprived in comparison with their colleagues), or from a commitment perspective (if it appears that a lack of organizational commitment plays a role; see Buunk & Ybema, 1997; Geurts, Buunk & Schaufeli, 1994a and b).

The Path from a Problem to a Problem Definition

The above delineates that a social psychologist seldom proceeds from a problem to a problem definition along a short, straight path. Rather, one travels a long and winding road and, along the way, there are a number of important decisions to be made. Some of them are quite straightforward. For instance, if bullying in the workplace is the focal problem, there is not much point in studying bullying among school children, except for comparative purposes perhaps.

Other decisions require a more careful consideration. Applied social scientists (and we are the first to admit this) all have their own hobby horses in terms of favourite topics and theories and will therefore see a particular problem in a particular way. For example, whereas an economist might stress the financial benefits of carpooling, a social psychologist might emphasize the benefits of carpooling in terms of companionship (Van Vugt, Van Lange, Meertens, & Joireman, 1996). In promoting contraceptive use, some social psychologists would pay more attention to the role of social cognitive factors in promoting contraceptive use (for example, a knowledge gap), whereas others would focus more on affective and motivational factors (for example, the desire to have unprotected sex; see Buunk, Bakker, Siero, van den Eijnden, 1998). It is good to be aware of such tendencies as they may colour a particular problem analysis (Kok, Schaalma, De Vries, Parcel and Paulussen, 1996).

In a related vein, when social psychologists are asked to get involved in solving a particular issue for a client, that client may not necessarily know exactly what the problem is or they may have a vested interest in defining a problem in a particular way. Take the example of the police service wanting to recruit ethnic officers. This force may be inclined to attribute past recruitment failures to a lack of interest from ethnic community members for police work rather than a reluctance by the police force to become more open and inclusive (cf. **fundamental attribution error**; Ross, 1977). Hence, a problem definition that would focus on persuading ethnic minority members to join would be less fruitful than a strategy directed at increasing tolerance among police officers. It is up to the social psychologist in question to make a judgment regarding the validity of a client's perspective and the reasons for defining a problem in a particular way. If a social psychologist believes that a client's perspective is not helpful, they should persuade him or her to adopt a different perspective and, if all else fails, should hand back the assignment to the client.

There are various reasons why it is important to develop a sound problem definition. First, it will delineate what needs to be explained and offer suggestions for finding the appropriate literature sources. On the basis of a good problem definition, it is easier to move to the next stage, the development and test of an explanatory model. Perhaps even more importantly, without a good problem orientation it is virtually impossible to map out a programme of interventions to tackle a problem. If a social psychologist fails to capture the essence of a problem, chances are that the proposed intervention programme will also fail. If, for example, the researcher wrongly assumes that company employees are interested in getting health checks done while at work, the provision of walk-in health centres near company premises will be a waste. The importance of problem definitions is illustrated below by various examples, both good and bad, of a hypothetical conversation between a social psychologist and a potential client, the chief constable of a large police force. The problem revolves around the recruitment of ethnic officers.

Examples of Interviews

Example of a Bad Interview

Chief: 'We are experiencing problems recruiting officers from Arab, Asian and African backgrounds into the police force. My colleagues in other police forces around the country tell me that they have the same problem.'

Social psychologist:	'What do you mean?'
Chief:	'Well, when we hold officer recruitment days for the public, hardly anyone from these communities turns up. And if they do, they don't submit the application form that they receive at the end of the day.'
Social psychologist:	'So, if I understand you correctly, you want to recruit more officers from an ethnic minority background.'
Chief:	'That's correct, but I also want to make sure that we retain our best ethnic officers. Quite a few of them have left recently, and we don't know why.'
Social psychologist:	'If I understand you correctly, the problem seems to be a lack of enthusiasm among the ethnic community for doing police work.'
Chief (hesitantly):	'Hm … yes, I believe so.'
Social psychologist:	'OK, I'll find some literature on job satisfaction and employee motivation and get back to you.'

Evaluation

In this example, the social psychologist and their client may decide to focus on understanding the lack of enthusiasm among ethnic officers for doing police work. Yet it is clear that they have developed, at best, an incomplete problem definition and, at worst, a problem definition that is plainly wrong. There are key questions that remain unanswered here. Is this a recruitment problem, a retention problem or is it both? For whom is it a problem – for the police, the community, the government? Is this really about a lack of interest in doing police work? Can the problem be attributed entirely to the ethnic community, or is the police force itself (also) responsible for causing these problems? Furthermore, when have these issues first been noticed, and if these problems have emerged only recently, how does that inform the search for possible causes? The next conversation provides a better example of the development of an adequate problem definition.

Example of a Better Interview

Chief:	'We are experiencing problems recruiting officers from Arab, Asian, and African backgrounds into the police force. My colleagues in other police forces around the country tell me that they have the same problem.'
Social psychologist:	'What seems to be the problem?'
Chief:	'Well, when we hold officer recruitment days for the public, hardly anyone from these communities turns up. And if they do, they don't submit the application form that they receive at the end of the day.'
Social psychologist:	'Why is this a problem?'
Chief:	'Well, there have been targets set by the government for the intake of ethnic officers, and so far, we have failed to reach any of these targets.'

Social psychologist:	'What is the relevance of these targets?'
Chief:	'We're operating in an ethnically diverse community, and it seems to us that the police force should be a fair reflection of the community in terms of its ethnic make-up.'
Social psychologist:	'Why is this important?'
Chief:	'We rely a lot on cooperation from the community in preventing and reporting crimes. At the moment, we're not getting this help. There's a lot of unreported crime in this area. When I talk to members of the public, particularly ethnic members, there seems to be a lot of suspicion about the police force.'
Social psychologist:	'What are these suspicions about?'
Chief:	'Some believe that we pay less attention to crimes when the victims are of Asian or African background. People also accuse us of being prejudiced in terms of who we stop and search on the streets.'
Social psychologist:	'So what is your main problem? That you are not recruiting enough ethnic police officers, that many crimes are unreported, or that some members of the community think the police are biased?'
Chief:	'All three really. But if we can do something about people's suspicions regarding our policing work, that would be a major step in the right direction.'
Social psychologist:	'So the main problem seems to be a lack of trust in the police force among the ethnic members of the community, which may or may not affect recruitment strategies – we don't know that yet. And you would like to know how trust can be improved?'
Chief:	'Yes, indeed.'

Evaluation

In this example, the problem definition is being shaped more clearly through the specific questions the social psychologist asks regarding the various attributes of the problem: *what* is the problem, *why* is it a problem and *for whom*? As a consequence, the problem has switched from specific recruitment to a more general issue regarding the relationship between the police force and ethnic community members.

It may seem that this is complicating matters unnecessarily. Yet think about the implications in terms of intervention. Had the social psychologist concentrated exclusively on the recruitment problem then he might have suggested organizing a recruitment campaign directly targeted at members of the ethnic population, for example, by advertising in mosques, temples or churches. Knowing that the recruitment failure might possibly result from a more widely held negative perception of the police force suggests that such an intervention is doomed to fail, because it does not directly alter the image of the police force. However, there are yet more issues to be raised by the social psychologist to establish a more complete problem definition.

Interview Continued

Social psychologist:	'Are there any other aspects to the problem'?
Chief:	'Over the past few years, I've also noticed an increase in turnover among ethnic officers, some of them were really the pick of the crop when they started here.'
Social psychologist:	'Do you know why they left the force?'
Chief:	'Well, we havn't done any systematic research, but some at least felt isolated in their working units. They didn't get enough support from colleagues in their units. They also felt under threat from members of their own community who didn't approve of them working for the police force.'
Social psychologist:	'Have you interviewed the chief officers in the units about the problems that the ethnic officers experienced?'
Chief:	'Not yet, I haven't had the time to go around the units and gather information.'
Social psychologist:	'But you think it's an important problem and that it may be related to what we previously mentioned, a lack of trust in the police force among the ethnic population.'
Chief:	'Keeping the best ethnic officers is paramount for our force. I think these problems are related, but, as I said before, where do we start?'
Social psychologist:	'What are your ideas about who best to focus our efforts on? Whose cooperation is necessary for the problem to be solved?'
Chief:	'Well, of course members of the ethnic community should be addressed. But in my opinion, a lot also depends on the chief unit officers. They talk on a daily basis with their officers and are responsible for the atmosphere in the unit. It is the task of the chief unit officer to stop bullying and discrimination among his officers.'
Social psychologist:	'So to summarize, we've now established that there are problems with regard to both the recruitment and the retention of ethnic police officers in this force. And improving recruitment and retention is important in order to increase the quality of police work in the community, and also importantly, to meet government targets. You see it as a priority in your force to tackle these problems. We don't know it for sure yet, but a possible cause of these problems may be a lack of trust in the police force among members of the ethnic population. This may prevent ethnic persons from applying to the force and it may promote the turnover of ethnic police officers. You believe that we should focus our efforts especially on members of the ethnic population and the chief unit officers. Is that a correct representation of what you said?'
Chief:	'Yes, I would agree with that analysis.'

Evaluation

This is a good start towards a workable, albeit preliminary, problem definition for a social psychologist. The problem definition is sufficiently concrete in terms of what the problems are (the recruitment and retention of ethnic police officers) and it suggests a possible cause for these problems (lack of trust in the police force). Furthermore, it addresses a number of questions relevant to establishing an adequate problem definition, such as:

1. *What is the problem*? The summary focuses on two (possibly related) problems in the force: the recruitment and retention of ethnic police officers.
2. *Why is it a problem*? In the summary, it becomes clear that these problems affect the quality of the police work in the community as well as the wider public image of the police force. Also, there is the issue about not meeting the government's ethnicity targets, which may result in the withdrawal of funds. It is not yet clear when these problems first appeared though.
3. *For whom is it a problem*? The social psychologist identifies at least four possible parties with an interest in solving these problems. First, the police force that wants to recruit more ethnic officers. Second, the community that wants a reliable and effective police force. Third, the ethnic members of the community who want to join/remain in the police force. And, finally, the government that wants police forces to meet their targets.
4. *What are the possible causes of the problem*? The social psychologist identifies one major cause of the problem in his summary, the lack of trust in the police force by members of the ethnic population. Although this may be a good working assumption for further examination, it is worthwhile realizing that there may be other causes as well. For example, the higher turnover among ethnic officers may be due to an inadequate support system within the police force for dealing with ethnicity. Or, it may turn out that ethnic officers are turned down more quickly for promotions. Finally, it may be that recruitment and retention failures are themselves the cause rather than the consequence of a lack of trust in the police. It is good to keep alternative causes in mind when building an explanatory model (see Chapter 3).
5. *What is the target group*? The social psychologist identifies those groups who, according to the chief, are essential for the success of a possible intervention, that is members of the ethnic population and the chief unit officers. Although this may be a good working assumption for further examination, it is worthwhile realizing that there may be other groups which need to be targeted as well. For instance, it seems wise to address all police officers, not just the chief unit officers. It is important to keep alternative target groups in mind when generating strategies and developing an intervention (see Chapter 5).
6. *What are the key aspects of the problem*?

   - Is it an applied problem? It is clear from the summary that the client – the police force – will not be satisfied if the social psychologist merely concentrates on finding the causes of the problems in recruitment and retention. They have asked for expert advice because they need to find solutions to these problems.
   - Is it a concrete problem? It seems rather obvious that the problem is concrete rather than abstract as it deals with specific groups and individuals.
   - Is it a social psychological problem? From the problem analysis it is clear that there are important social psychological dimensions to the problem. Underlying these problems are potential issues of trust, prejudice, **social support**, power and legitimacy – all social psychological phenomena. Also, there will be important social psychological aspects to

the proposed intervention programme, such as trust-building, reducing prejudice, and increasing the legitimacy of the police force.
- Can the problem be solved or relieved? From the above, it appears that there are enough clues to reassure the social psychologist that the problems are solvable or relievable, at least in principle. Moreover, there is clearly a willingness on the part of the client to work towards reducing the problem.

It is good to note that the above list is by no means an exhaustive list of questions that could be asked in order to develop an adequate problem definition. There are many other issues that could be raised by the social psychologist in order to get a clearer picture of the problem. For example, it is not entirely clear from the interview when these problems first emerged or exactly when they were first noted by the Chief Constable (part of the *why* question). It may be that recruitment failure is a long-standing issue, but that it has only been noticed recently by the Chief in response to feedback about the government targets. Or it may be a relatively recent phenomenon, perhaps caused by particular incidents where ethnic community members have been treated badly and unjustly by some police officers, thus raising a negative image of the police. Such an historic analysis is important because it sheds further light on the potential causes of the problem. Also, the social psychologist did not explore further the remark made by the Chief that the problem had been observed in other police forces as well. Establishing whether this is true or not may help to build a more complete picture of the problem, as well as providing an opportunity to study interventions that may have been tried elsewhere.

A good preliminary problem definition is one in which all the relevant questions have been addressed, but in no obvious order. We will focus below on the specific questions that need to be addressed to develop a problem definition. It is possible that there will be some overlap in the answers to each of these questions. That is not a problem. At this stage, omissions are greater sins than overlaps. Further, as we noted earlier, it is important not to get fixated on one particular cause or explanation (for example, in this case trust in the police force). A good social psychologist should always leave open the possibility of adjusting the problem definition, once he or she gets under way in building an explanatory model, collecting literature and conducting research.

KEY QUESTIONS FOR A PROBLEM DEFINITION

What is the Problem?

The main issue here is what is the central problem that needs to be understood and resolved? To answer this question requires an insight into the cause and background of the problem. With many problem definitions it is not always clear what the crux of the problem is. A conversation with a potential client may lead to a somewhat distorted version of the nature and background of the problem. In the previous example, the Chief Constable may have had a vested interest in assuming that a failure to recruit ethnic police officers was due to a lack of interest within the community rather than a lack of effort from the force. A social psychologist therefore needs to be both critical towards anything that a client says and also open-minded about what the true causes of a particular problem might be.

A few years ago, one of the authors of this book was asked by the board of a water company to examine residential water use and conservation attitudes during a shortage. Some initial research was carried out, which revealed that residents with a water meter acted much more responsibly in response to the shortage than residents without a meter (Van Vugt, 1999; Van Vugt & Samuelson, 1999). In presenting his findings, he suggested that the problem should be refocused on how to get residents to voluntarily adopt water meters. This problem definition did not agree with that of the board of the water company, who did not want to introduce widespread metering because of the costs involved. Instead, the board wanted to focus on changing the conservation attitudes of those households without meters.

Another concern is that problems are often stated in terms that are too generic to be useful. For example, suppose a council officer notices that there is a lot of litter in certain areas within a city. He also observes that many people are using cars to drive their children to school. He therefore concludes that the residents are not environmentally conscious enough and asks a social psychologist to look into strategies to make people more environmentally aware. Yet the stated problem 'residents are not environmentally aware' is probably too general to be of much use in finding strategies to solve the problem. Indeed, an anti-littering campaign would probably emphasize the norm that one ought not to litter, but in anti-car campaigns such **normative** pressures are likely to be [KT] ineffective (Cialdini, Kallgren & Reno, 1991; Van Vugt et al., 1996).

Why is it a Problem?

It is important for social psychologists to ask why a particular issue is perceived as a problem in the first place. How does the problem express itself? What are the consequences of the problem? What makes it problematic? When did it first emerge? If the vice-chancellor of a university approaches a social psychologist with a question on what to do about university drop out rates, they must first establish why it is a problem that some students do not finish their studies. Is it largely a financial matter for the university, or is there (also) a concern about the self-esteem and well-being of such students? Furthermore, if the vice-chancellor believes it has something to do with the 'motivation' of particular students, the social psychologist should ask them to specify what they mean by this rather abstract term. Is it a question of them not attending lectures (in which case compulsory attendance may be considered) or did they have the wrong expectations about the study or university life in general (leading to an intervention to alter prospective students' course expectations)? Thus, answering the *why* question does not just help to specify the problem, it also suggests directions for the proposed intervention programme.

It may take some effort to find out which problems really bother a client. A first impression about the Chief Constable is that he is concerned with meeting the targets set by the government about the intake of ethnic officers. This may indeed be an immediate concern, but it is only after further enquiry that the social psychologist finds out that it is really the quality of police functioning and a lack of cooperation from the community that concern him. If the problem is solely defined in terms of meeting targets then the success of interventions will be based on this criterion. This may not necessarily be desirable in the long run. In the police example, the force may use substantial incentives to recruit ethnic officers in order to meet the intake targets, but new recruits may not have the right attitude and motivation to continue in the job, eventually dropping out. Hence, it is vital not to be persuaded by the quick-fix solutions that clients themselves may offer by simply looking at their perspective on the problem. Equally, however, one should be careful to define the problem entirely within the subjects' interests. For example, ethnic police officer recruits should be subject to the same stringent criteria for admission into the force and should therefore not be seen as getting an easy ride (Heilman, Simon & Repper, 1987; Maio & Esses, 1998).

To answer the why question, it may help to ask since when it was a problem. This might reveal important clues about the potential causes and solutions of the problem. By asking these questions a social psychologist attempts to build an historical picture of the problem, which can be quite informative. First, it can reveal that what appears to be a problem may not necessarily be a problem after all. For example, sales of the 'morning-after' pill at chemists around the country may appear to be rising, but a brief investigation may reveal that this is really due to the government being able to give a more precise sales figure for the first time. Second, an historical analysis might point to a particular time when the problem first started to emerge or be noticed. For example, citizens and nations first started to become aware of issues regarding environmental conservation after the oil crisis in 1972, when oil-producing countries cut their supplies (Gardner & Stern, 1996). Similarly, the drought in England in the summer of 1995 made English people suddenly aware of the finiteness of important water supplies. Knowing this might help a social psychologist to propose an intervention programme using the **salience** of this crisis (Van Vugt, 1999; Van Vugt & Samuelson, 1999). Third, a brief historical analysis may indicate reasons why a problem has suddenly increased in severity. For example, the sudden rise in sales of the 'morning-after' pill at chemists may be due to the difficulty some underage teenagers have in getting the contraceptive pill from their doctor without parental consent.

Of course, it is also possible that the issue has been ongoing for a much longer time, but suddenly has been perceived as a problem by the client because of some ulterior reason. It is important to be aware of this. The Chief Constable in the police example may have known about the recruitment failure of ethnic officers for a long time, but only been willing to consider it a genuine problem because of the intake targets recently set by the Government. If a social psychologist is unaware of this, he or she may be tempted to propose a quick-fix solution to the problem rather than one that would prove successful in the long term.

For Whom is it a Problem?

Who are the parties involved in the problem? It is instructive to know whether the problem involves just the client or whether there are also other parties involved. The latter is usually the case. The recruitment failure in the example is of concern not just to the chief (who may lose his job if targets are not met) or the force (which may face a financial penalty), but also to those members of the community who wish to join the force, and even of concern to the entire community itself (namely, if there is a lack of trust in the police, the community welfare may be at risk: see Tyler & Blader, 2002; Van Vugt et al., 2000). A subsequent step is to ask oneself if the other parties perceive the problem in the same way. It may be instructive to spend some time investigating this. Often it will emerge that parties agree about the problem definition. However, we should not automatically assume that this is the case. As an extreme illustration, one of the authors of this book was asked by the chair of a professional football club to investigate why the club's youth academy was not producing enough first team players. In a subsequent interview with the director of the youth academy, he plainly denied that such a problem existed and pointed to evidence which contradicted the chairman's claims. It is obvious that these contrasting perspectives made it very difficult for the social psychologist to accept this assignment.

Sometimes, involved parties will notice the existence of a problem but they may not necessarily agree on the kind of problem they face. The more complex problems are, the more likely this seems to be the case. For example, the managing director of a firm may believe that the cause of absenteeism in the company is a lack of monitoring of workers by supervisors. However, an interview with the workers may reveal an entirely different picture. They may perceive their absences as being caused by extensive control and policing by their supervisors. If problems are defined so differently by the parties involved, this is in itself a problem. In such cases, before engaging in any further work, a social psychologist must consult with all the parties involved to agree on a version of the problem that all can endorse.

Finally, it is significant to note that even actors within the same party may have a different version of the story. For example, in a firm where some female employees feel discriminated against, it is good to find out if all females in the company experience these problems in the same way. Only through interviews with several members of the party involved can a social psychologist develop an adequate problem definition, incorporating the multitude of perspectives that exist about the origins of the problem.

What are the Possible Causes of the Problem?

With this question a social psychologist can build up a picture of the background to and potential causes of the problem. He can also determine if there is a social psychological dimension to the problem, and if so, can use this to create a preliminary causal model (see Chapter 3). Note that the purpose of establishing a problem definition is not to be definite about the exact causes underlying the problem. At this stage, it is more important to get a first impression of the causal model and the possible social psychological processes involved.

Building a preliminary causal model is facilitated by asking two interrelated questions:

1. What causes this problem?
2. How do these causes affect the problem?

In the volunteering example, the Nottingham charity experienced difficulties in recruiting volunteers and they attributed this problem to a potential cause, which is that people nowadays have many other commitments. Suppose this is true, how would this cause then affect the problem? A straightforward causal explanation would be that because people nowadays work at the weekend more, they will have less time to engage in other activities, such as volunteering.

It is also important at this point to distinguish between *immediate* causes and more *distal* causes. By making this distinction, one can develop a model of the causal process leading to the problem. For example, the Chief Constable conveyed that the force was failing to recruit ethnic officers and noticed an immediate cause of the problem: members of ethnic groups simply not attending officer recruitment days in large numbers. The social psychologist then has to delve deeper into this problem by asking what causes this. Suppose the chief suggested that ethnic community members have little interest in joining the police and suffer from a lack of motivation. The social psychologist should then ask why this might be the case and the Chief Constable might answer that there is a lack of trust in the police force among the ethnic community. What causes this? Perhaps they feel that the police are prejudiced against their community. Why may this be the case? The chief might then reveal a number of high-profile incidents whereby crimes against the ethnic population, including some racial crimes, were never solved. He may also point to the failure of current ethnic officers to get promotion, which may have caused grievances in the population. A process-like causal model now emerges leading all the way from unresolved racial crimes (a distant cause), to the failure to recruit ethnic officers, with a number of more immediate causes in between (accusations of prejudice, a lack of trust in the police, a lack of motivation to do police work).

Establishing the process of events reveals a number of different clues about the causal model underlying the problem as well as the proposed intervention programme to tackle it. Nevertheless, at this stage it may not be clear what exactly the causal chain of events leading to the problem is or which factors play a major or minor role in causing the problem. This is not a worry. In the next steps of the model it will become clear what the causal model looks like through further research and theorizing. And yet, the factors that have been identified in the problem definition could certainly play a role in choosing the theories to develop the causal model.

What is the Target Group?

Even though we are in the earliest stage of defining our problem, a social psychologist should already get some idea of the target group. Whom should be convinced of the problem? Whose cooperation is necessary for the problem to be solved? In the police example, a social psychologist may decide to bring it to the attention of police officers and try to influence their attitudes. He may approach members of the ethnic community, especially those between 20 and 30 years old, and encourage them to apply for a place in the police force, or he may do both. He may even focus his efforts on Members of Parliament, and try to persuade them to lower the strict targets the government has set for the intake of ethnic officers.

Selecting a target group narrows down the broad field of actors that may play a role in the problem. It clarifies the problem and makes it more specific. This in turn makes it easier to come up with strategies to help solve the problem (see Chapter 5). Should the social psychologist later discover that the target group is too difficult or costly to aim his intervention at, he can always backtrack and redefine the problem. Remember, the PATH model is not a rigid process and going from problem to intervention is usually an iterative process that includes moving back and forth between the different steps in the model.

What are the Key Aspects of the Problem?

To capture the main aspects of the problem, social psychologists have to ask to what extent the problem is a) an *applied* problem; b) a *concrete* problem; c) a *social psychological* problem; and d) to what extent the problem can be *dealt with*.

Is it an Applied Problem?

Many problem definitions set by psychologists are concerned only with finding the causes for a particular problem, for example, what gene is responsible for aggression? These fundamental research problems are very important but they are not the kind of problems we are interested in here. The issues we are interested in, and this should be clear by now, are those that require an intervention to be developed. Finding an effective solution to a problem is not the primary concern of fundamental research in psychology, but it is the priority of most applied psychological research. Nevertheless, even in applied research there is a distinction between research questions that primarily focus on finding the causes of a particular problem, like divorce, burn-out, racism, or environmental pollution, and questions that are directed toward finding solutions (for example, how can we tackle racism?).

In this regard, it is important that the 'why is it a problem?' question also incorporates a question about the way a particular problem could be solved. Because it is not always clear at the beginning what the intervention programme will look like, some problem definitions are merely stated in terms of identifying the cause of the problem (for example, why do police forces find it difficult to recruit ethnic officers?). To frame it in this way, however, would be a mistake because the ultimate goal of the problem task is to actually do something about the issue (namely, how to recruit more ethnic officers). It is important not to forget this when designing a problem definition because it provides a standard against which any work done by the social psychologist will be evaluated .

Thus an example of a good problem definition would be: 'Why does the police force find it difficult to recruit ethnic officers, and what can be done to increase the intake of ethnic officers'? This is not to imply that the problem then immediately shifts towards searching for a quick-fix solution. It is only by building a good causal model of the problem using social psychological theory and research that a social psychologist will be able to suggest an intervention programme that is likely to succeed. Only by finding out exactly why there is a lack of interest from the ethnic community in joining this police force can a coherent programme of intervention be put together.

Is it a Concrete Problem?

It is also important that the problem is formulated in sufficiently concrete terms. All its important aspects must be operationalized appropriately if they are to be useful. For example, a problem definition aimed at doing something about bullying in the workplace should try to define bullying in a manner which makes it sufficiently clear to everyone what it means, such as 'the act of intimidating a less powerful person into doing something against their wish' (see the Wordnet definition at http://wordnet.princeton.edu/). Once the behaviour has been operationalized, it is much easier to recognize it and measure the frequency of bullying behaviour in the workplace.

Furthermore, it is sensible to specify the properties of the particular sample of people who experience or cause the problem in as much detail as possible. Rather than stating the problem as 'the failure to recruit ethnic officers', one could specify the backgrounds of the potential recruits the force is looking for (for example, officers of Pakistani and Indian descent). This makes it easier to find out if an intervention has been successful or not.

Finally, one should be clear in the problem definition about the kind of specific behaviours that one wants to tackle with an intervention. A problem concerning the anti-social behaviour of teenagers in urban neighbourhoods can only be dealt with if a social psychologist has not only defined the behaviour, but also has a clear indication of the specific behaviours that fit within the general domain of anti-social behaviour. This could include such diverse acts as littering, graffiti, vandalism, joy-riding or verbal and/or physical aggression against other children or adults. Only by being clear about the set of behaviours is a social psychologist able to develop and test the effectiveness of an intervention programme.

To encourage specifying the problem, a social psychologist is advised to step into the shoes of a researcher. Suppose you are asked to develop a research programme measuring bullying in the workplace – how would you measure this behaviour? What questions would you ask the employees in the company that you are investigating, and what behaviours would you be interested in observing? You may decide that you are interested primarily in finding out whether male employees make any derogatory comments about female colleagues or about females in general in the presence of other staff. In order to do this, you may decide to interview staff members and get permission to record conversations and email exchanges between staff members. Once you have established the prevalence of the problem, you may suggest a possible intervention to the client (for example, informing staff that email traffic will be monitored). Because you have specified the bullying problem that you are interested in, you can then go on to measure the effectiveness of this intervention.

Is it a Social Psychological Problem?

This question will have been addressed, at least in part, by answers to the previous questions. There are two related concerns here. Are there any causes other than social psychological causes of the problem, and, if there are, are these perhaps more important than the social psychological determinants? For example, there is little point in asking a social psychologist to solve a shortage of hospital beds because this is largely a financial and administrative matter. Similarly, if we know that the major factor influencing residential water use is the presence of a water meter, a social psychologist can do little in terms of social psychological interventions to influence people to conserve more water (Van Vugt, 1999).

A second, related, question is what contribution a social psychological perspective on the problem could make, especially in relation to other perspectives such as an economic, political, or engineering perspective. Of primary interest to social psychologists are problems that are associated with how individuals behave and respond to their social environments. If problems are primarily an issue of money (say, hospital beds), politics (for example, EU laws), or technology (say, cleaner energy sources), then a social psychological approach is likely to be ineffective. Similarly, if a problem is primarily clinical (for example, anorexia among young females) or cognitive (say, improving performance on intelligence tests), there is also less need for social psychological expertise.

But the same problem can be looked at from different angles, only one of them being a social psychological angle. For example, in studying the origins of anti-social behaviour among teenagers one could take a social psychological perspective, examining how such activities are informed by peer pressure and a conformity to social norms. A psychological problem orientation would involve looking at whether there were differences between teenagers in their preparedness to engage in anti-social behaviour that could be explained by facets of someone's personality (for example, extraversion, agreeableness). Similarly, one could take a developmental-psychological view, examining ontogenetic differences between teenagers who engage in anti-social behaviours versus those who do not. Finally, one may be interested primarily in the societal causes underlying anti-social behaviour among teenagers, for example, understanding the relationship between anti-social behaviour and age, family income, type of housing or the professions of parents. Each of these perspectives helps to foster an understanding of the problem and, in collaboration with other social science disciplines, social psychology provides an essential part of the problem analysis.

However, the primary input on a problem from a social psychologist will be the extent to which the issue is caused by aspects of the social environment: what is the effect of individuals' social interactions on the development of the problem and its possible solution? Even within this broader social psychological framework, different sub-perspectives can be recognized. A distinction is usually made between three perspectives: the social self, **social cognition**, and social interaction (see, for example, Aronson, Wilson & Akert, 2005; Brehm, Kassin & Fein, 2005; Hewstone, Stroebe & Jonas, 2005; Hogg & Vaughan, 2005; Kenrick, Neuberg & Cialdini, 2005; Myers, 2005). In the police example, a social interaction expert will emphasize the importance of the quality of the relationships between the force and the ethnic community as an underlying cause of the recruitment problems (Tyler & Smith, 1998). The social cognition expert will pay more attention to how the parties perceive each other (Fiske, 1998), for example, do police officers hold any prejudiced beliefs about ethnic officers or the ethnic population in general? Finally, an expert from the social self perspective would perhaps focus more on the effects of felt prejudice on the self-esteem of ethnic officers (Baumeister, 1999). Yet it must be stressed that these are merely differences in emphasis. A well-equipped applied social psychologist should be able to employ theories and techniques from the entire social psychological toolkit.

Box 2.2   A Case Study: The Modification of Driving Behaviour in a Large Transport Organization

The depletion of fossil fuels is a huge problem facing the world. Traditional energy sources, such as oil, are being used up at an increasing rate, and, as a consequence, become more expensive. Alternative sources of energy need to be developed, but that takes time. For now, saving energy is therefore of vital importance. Social psychologist Sjef Siero and his colleagues at the University of Groningen (The Netherlands) were asked by The Netherlands Postal and Telecommunications Services (PTT) to develop an intervention programme to change the driving behaviour of mail-van drivers so as to encourage energy savings.*

The social psychologists first conducted a pilot study to identify the determinants of the driving behaviour of the mail-van drivers. A questionnaire was sent to 628 drivers that contained questions about the drivers' driving styles, beliefs about the possible consequences of energy-saving driving, the opinions of colleagues and superiors (social norms), and the PTT organization.

Results from this pilot showed that thrifty drivers differed from wasteful drivers with respect to several beliefs, social norms, and organization-related variables. For instance, drivers who shift gears at a higher number of revolutions (RPM) and thus drive more wastefully, generally believe that the motor will become lazy if gears are shifted at a lower RPM. On the basis of these results, an intervention programme was designed that incorporated three interventions to influence driving behaviour: providing information about economical driving styles, appointing local supervisors to control the drivers' gasoline consumption, and providing drivers with feedback on their gasoline consumption.

In a field experiment in a postal district the social psychologists studied the effect of the intervention programme. Their study showed that, compared to a control group, mail-van drivers in the experimental group (who received the intervention) reported more positive attitudes and social norms towards economic driving and had adopted a more economic driving style. As a result, energy savings of more than 7 per cent were achieved.

* Siero, S., Boon, M., Kok, G. & Siero, F. (1989). Modification of driving behaviour in a large transport organisation: A field experiment. *Journal of Applied Psychology, 74,* 417–423.

Is the Problem Solvable?

A final issue that should be mentioned here is the judgement by a social psychologist about whether a problem, which has been analysed carefully in terms of its social psychological aspects, can be solved or, at least, substantially relieved. A careful analysis of the viability of several possible solutions is important because it could avoid a lot of frustration on the part of both client and social psychologist if they find out that the intervention they have chosen is simply impractical or socially undesirable.

For example, based on the suggestion from the social psychological expert, a company may develop an excellent carrot-and-stick plan to promote cycling by building safe bike racks, showers, and reducing the number of car parking spaces. But if it then turns out that most employees live more than 10 miles from work it becomes a very impractical solution indeed. Employees may feel deprived of something which they think they are entitled to and may experience anger and resentment as a consequence (a phenomenon called '**relative deprivation**'; see Buunk, Zurriaga, Gonzalez-Roma & Subirats, 2003; Walker & Smith, 2002).

KT

In a similar vein, what would seem to be the most efficient solution to the problem may not be the one that a client want or likes to hear. Recall here the story about the water shortages in which water meters were identified by the social psychologist as the best possible solution to reduce water use, but due to cost this solution was not much favoured by the board of the water company (Van Vugt, 1999).

Particular interventions, however attractive they seem at first glance, should also be avoided on ethical grounds. For example, probably the easiest way to get more ethnic officers in the police force is by lowering the tough selection standards for this particularly group of recruits. One wonders though whether such affirmative action policies are morally defensible and whether they are good for the individual officer as well. There is evidence, for example, which suggests that employees who enter a job via an affirmative action programme have a miserable working life because they are thus stigmatized at work (Heilman et al., 1987). Thus, social psychologists must think very carefully when establishing a problem definition which includes a suggestion to improve a particular situation (which most good problem definitions do) and as to whether the interventions that are likely to be the most effective in theory will also be possible to implement in practice. Only via thorough analysis of the problem and interviews with the client and various other parties will it be revealed if this is the case or not.

RESEARCH FOR A PROBLEM DEFINITION

To answer any questions pertaining to a sound problem definition, it is often necessary to conduct some preliminary research by collecting data from multiple sources. The primary aim of research in this phase is to better understand the problem and its possible causes as well as to estimate the feasibility of potential interventions. At this stage, we are not yet concerned with an empirical test of the causal model nor with an evaluation of the intervention programme. Nevertheless, some exploratory research could be helpful because it might generate ideas regarding the antecedents of the problem, and provide valuable clues for what the intervention may look like. The interview with the Chief Constable mentioned previously can be viewed as an example of preliminary data gathering by the social psychologist.

Exploratory research is often desirable for establishing the problem definition because it ensures that the social psychologist does not make any mistakes in identifying the primary causes of or solutions to the problem. For example, in order to facilitate doctors' visits among people with long working hours (problem), the government intends to build walk-in health centres near main industrial zones (solution). Yet a preliminary investigation into the feasibility of this intervention may reveal that employees are reluctant to use this opportunity because they will not get time off work from their employer. Or alternatively, from interviewing employees a social psychologist may conclude that the option is not attractive because employees are fearful about their privacy if they visit a doctor at or near their workplace. Thus, a considerable amount of time and money could be saved by conducting preliminary research into the endorsement of particular intervention programmes.

There may be constraints in conducting research at such an early stage in the relationship between client and social psychologist. Clients may not yet know whether they would want to use the services of a social psychologist so they may be reluctant to give permission to them to gather data. Or the problem or intervention may still be confidential, and therefore it may be too sensitive to collect data, for example, by interviewing interested parties. Nevertheless, a social psychologist should try to conduct a preliminary investigation into the problem in order to establish a sound problem definition and ensure that relevant information is not ignored. There are various sources available to collect preliminary information about a problem.

Background Materials

For some social problems there may be a variety of materials already available to the social psychologist. Bigger social issues (for example, poverty, crime, anti-terror policies) usually appear in newspapers or on television and it would be worthwhile to inspect these media for information about a particular problem. In addition, it is always sensible to do a search on the internet – the largest database of all – for information. For us, as authors of this book, the internet will often be the first port of call if we need to read about a particular issue.

The facts and figures surrounding a specific problem may be readily available. For example, if one wants to inspect crime figures in a particular area one should consult the statistics that are available from the local police or government. In general, national and local governments are a great source of information on all sorts of matters and it would be advisable to contact them with specific requests.

Finally, it is advisable not to rely exclusively on information that has come directly from a client as this may often be incomplete. In the police example, the Chief Constable may have had information regarding the percentage of ethnic officers currently in the force, but he may not necessarily have known how many had been turned down after they had applied. Similarly, relying on a client as the sole source of information may give a somewhat distorted picture of the problem. The Chief Constable may have ascertained that in the past recruitment efforts had been specifically designed to recruit ethnic officers, but present day interviews with potential and current ethnic applicants may now reveal that they believe that they have not received any special attention from the force. To gain more insight into a problem, it is therefore important to rely on a number of different sources to obtain background knowledge of a particular issue.

Scientific Literature

It may also be instructive to conduct a brief review of the available scientific literature at this point. Although a more systematic literature review will be done at a later stage, it is good to know what information is out there in order to facilitate the search for potential problem causes and solutions. Going back to the example of threatening and abusive teenagers, a brief summary of the social psychological literature may provide a wealth of data that can give a valuable insight into the problem of aggression among children. A closer scrutiny of the literature could be made by consulting PsychINFO, PsychARTICLES or Google SCHOLAR (electronic databases that comprise all scientific articles and books in the field of psychology between 1872 and today). An investigation of these sources may, for instance, reveal that:

1. Boys are more aggressive than girls.
2. Aggression is more common in so-called cultures of honour.
3. The literature distinguishes between instrumental aggression, that is aggression to achieve a goal, and emotional aggression, that is aggression that stems from anger and frustration.
4. Violence is often associated with alcohol intake.
5. The hotter it is on any given day, the more common violence is.
6. The presence of an 'aggressive' object, such as a knife or baseball bat, increases people's aggression if they are provoked.
7. Children can learn aggression by watching violence on television or in video games.
8. Punishment decreases aggression if the punishment is prompt and certain.
9. Aggression can be reduced by improving communication skills.

A closer scrutiny of the literature may also yield a number of additional perspectives and explanations that could shed further light on the prevalence of anti-social behaviour and aggression among youngsters. These may be used to develop hypotheses about the causal model and, ultimately, to set up a plan for intervention. In the problem phase, the main purpose is to generate as many ideas as possible about the possible antecedents of the problem, which would facilitate the establishment of a causal model to develop later on.

Interviews

It is good to talk. Even though there may be plenty of background and scientific materials available on a particular issue, it is always good practice to organize interviews with those individuals who are party to a particular problem (the *for whom* question). This helps to get an intuitive understanding of the problem, which is not as easy to get from studying the literature alone. Interviews also enable social psychologists to get a better picture about how the parties experience their problems and, importantly, whether they view matters in a similar or in a different way. Only through interviews can a problem definition be developed that all parties recognize and are willing to sign up to.

In general, it is advisable to interview the members of all relevant parties, that is, those who experience the problem, those who may cause the problem, and those who are responsible for solving the problem. In the latter category, one should interview the key figures in an organization who are responsible for finding solutions to the problem. In the police example, the social psychologist had already interviewed the Chief Constable, but it would also be advisable in this case to interview the key staff members who are responsible for recruitment and training. They may be part of the problem, but even if they are they may have valuable observations and insights to offer. In addition, the social psychologist here may want to approach the chief constables of other forces to find out if they are experiencing a similar problem.

It is, of course, equally important to interview people who are affected by the problem and have experienced the negative consequences themselves. In the above example, these would be those ethnic officers who have left the police force (or are thinking about leaving) and the ethnic members of the community who have an interest in doing police work or in other examples, those teenagers who have been the victims of anti-social behaviour. The perpetrators of bullying must be interviewed by the social psychologist concerned.

These initial interviews ought to have a number of important features in order to be useful. First, they must be relatively unstructured as they should enable the interviewer plenty of room to interact freely with the interviewees based upon what they raise. Unstructured interviews are the best way to gather information at this stage of the investigation. One would only need a checklist of different topics and questions to use as a guideline for the interview. The rigorous scientific standards of objectivity and reliability do not apply as much to this stage of data collection as they do to the more advanced stages of this methodology. This is not to say that just about anything can be raised in these interviews, but it is important not to be too prejudiced about certain explanations or interpretations that interviewees might bring up. Even a rather unlikely explanation should not be dismissed a priori. If the interviewee believes it then he or she will judge any problem definition or intervention in terms of dealing with the explanation they offer. For example, the Chief Constable may prove genuinely convinced that members of ethnic populations are not very interested in conducting police work full stop. Although this may be proven to be untrue at a later stage, he will most likely not accept a problem definition that excludes this as a possibility.

Another feature of these interviews is to investigate if there are differences between interested parties in their perspectives on a problem. If all parties perceive the problem in the same way, it will be much easier to solve the problem. However, the mere fact that they have hired a social psychologist to intervene suggests that the different parties may have a different version of what has caused the problem. Interviewers should be focused on detecting these differences as they provide useful information. For instance, the social psychologist who investigates the lack of enthusiasm for doing volunteer work at a charity would interview not only the board of the charity, but also current and former volunteers. After an initial impression from the charity board that people are 'simply too busy to want to get involved in charity work these days' the social psychologist might become a bit more sceptical about this version of events when they had interviewed current and ex-volunteers who indicated that:

1. the charity needs to raise more money to be successful (which partly answers the *what* is the problem question);
2. the charity has just replaced its director (which partly answers the issue for *whom* it is a problem);
3. there are conflicts between the paid staff and volunteer staff members (which partly answers the question regarding the *causes* of the problem);
4. the charity has not made any major recruitment efforts (which partly answers whether the problem *is solvable*);
5. the charity has approached the wrong people (*target group*) to volunteer, that is mainly students and working mothers. Although they might want to, both students and working mothers are generally just too busy to do volunteer work.

Observation

Sometimes it can be difficult to work towards a problem definition by collecting material from interviews alone. Interviewees may have such different views on a problem that it will be extremely difficult to generate a problem definition that is universally agreed upon. Equally, it is possible that there can appear to be a sense of unanimity among interviewees about a problem, but the social psychologist involved is a bit suspicious about whether everyone is telling the entire truth. Some issues, such as institutional racism or sexual harassment in the workplace, are so sensitive to deal with that it may be in the interests of all parties to hide important information in the interviews. In such cases, a social psychologist may want to rely on an indirect method, such as observation, to gather more reliable data about a specific issue.

There are various methods of observation that may be informative in establishing a problem definition. First, one could rely on a more unstructured observation method where no formal observation and coding scheme is necessary. As with the interviews, one could prepare a checklist of different topics that one would like to pay attention to in a particular setting. For example, in studying anti-social behaviour among youngsters it may be helpful to go into the neighbourhoods in which these youngsters live and actually observe their social interactions. In studying household recycling, one could observe and analyse the contents of recyclable and non-recyclable bags to see what people put in them – which is what we did in a recent project (Lyas, Shaw & Van Vugt, 2002). In companies with high levels of absenteeism, it may be relevant to have a look around the workplace to investigate under what conditions employees do their work and to what extent absenteeism is accepted in work teams (Buunk, 1990).

Sometimes it is better to remain unidentified as a social psychologist. The classic Hawthorne effect tells us that people behave differently when they realize that they are being watched (for example, *Big Brother*; see also Gillespie, 1991). This is particularly important in the study of more sensitive social issues, such as racial prejudice and sexual harassment. For example, in a classic study on prejudice (LaPiere, 1934), a team of researchers in the USA contacted various motels and hotels across the country by pretending to be interested in renting a room. The white researcher had a much higher success rate in getting the room than the Chinese researcher, perhaps an indication of prejudice. It is quite clear that had the research team relied on interview data it would have been rather unlikely that the home owners would have expressed any open signs of prejudice. Naturally, the success of this participant observation technique stands or falls with the quality of fit between the researcher's profile and the profile of the sample he/she is studying.

Box 2.3 Examples of Good Problem Definitions

Below are two examples of problem definitions that social psychologists may come up with after answering the six key questions (see Box 2.4) and gathering additional data about the problem through interviews and observation, thus collecting background and scientific materials about the problem.

Example 1: Littering in Birmingham city centre

Littering is a problem in many larger cities in Europe and the USA (Gardner & Stern, 1996). Many inner-city residents in Birmingham see it as a nuisance and have complained to the city council about the amount of litter they find on their streets (the *who* and *why* questions), especially at the weekends (the *what* question). It is an ongoing problem, but people are more aware of it now that more people have started living in the city centre. The council is reluctant to hire more street cleaners because of the extra costs involved (the *who* and *why* questions). The main question now is how street littering can be prevented in the centre of Birmingham (the *what* question). This is an applied problem that can potentially be solved after an intervention (*problem aspects*). The problem is specific in so far as it needs to be tackled in Birmingham (the *target group* question), but the results may have implications for anti-littering strategies elsewhere (*problem aspects*).

There is likely to be a social psychological dimension to the problem (*problem aspects*). The literature suggests that people litter more if they see others doing it (Cialdini et al., 1991) and when they think they can get away with it, for instance at night (the *cause* question). They may also think that it is not their responsibility to clean it up (the *cause* question). It is possible that the problem is aggravated by a lack of street bins in the centre (the *cause* question). The problem might be tackled through an intervention (psychological and/or infrastructural), although it is questionable whether the problem can be completely solved.

Example 2: Obesity among school children in the UK

According to government statistics in Britain, almost one in 10 children in the UK is now seriously overweight, and if nothing is done this figure is likely to rise (see http://www.nationalobesityforum.org.uk/). Obesity is a problem (the *what* question) as it is linked to a number of health problems, such as high blood pressure, heart and kidney problems and diabetes, which lower the life expectancy of these individuals (the *who* question) and lead to a rise in the costs of health care for the nation as a whole (the *why* and *who* questions). Obese children are also more likely to be stigmatized at school (the *who* question), and as a consequence may suffer from underachievement and, more generally, a low self-esteem (the *why* question; see Crandall, 1988).

As preventing obesity seems to be easier than tackling it after it has emerged in children, the main question is how obesity can be prevented in children (the *what* question). Although there are basic questions that still need to be answered regarding the causes of obesity, the problem is applied. Obesity is caused by many different factors, but it most certainly involves unhealthy eating habits and a lack of exercise (the *cause* question). Unhealthy eating and a lack of exercise are two behaviours that have a clear social psychological dimension, because they are influenced by, among other factors, prevailing social norms, peer pressure, and modelling by parents (*problem aspects*). The *target group* constitutes at a minimum obese children and their parents. As obesity is such a complex problem, it is likely best tackled through a mix of interventions, including incentives, infrastructural arrangements and social psychological intervention.

COMPLETING THE PROBLEM DEFINITION

Having collected all the relevant information through consulting different sources in order to answer the key questions, we can now formulate the problem definition. A problem definition usually consists of a single paragraph that articulates the key properties of the problem in a fluent and coherent manner. A problem definition is not a laundry list of answers to different questions, although initially it is better to systematically address each question to make sure they have all been discussed. Answers, of course, are not just phrased as simple statements like 'Yes, this is a social psychological problem'. Each answer should carefully explain why: 'This is a social psychological problem, because bullying is about the relationship between a powerful and less powerful person'. It should be clear from the final problem definition what the problem is, why it is a problem, for whom it is a problem, what are the main causes, the target group and relevant problem aspects. Box 2.3 contains a few examples of good problem definitions.

We must stress that for educational purposes we would recommend that researchers initially develop the problem definition by answering systematically all the key questions on the list. Later on, once the researcher has gained experience working with our methodology, they can prepare a longer version for themselves and an abbreviated version for a client. This shorter version would usually describe what the problem is, why it is a problem, for whom it is a problem, and the background and potential causes of the problem.

Box 2.4   The Problem Phase: Steps From A Problem To A Problem Definition

In reaching a solid problem definition you need to address the following questions (not necessarily in the order below). In so doing, you will have to gather data about the problem by collecting background information, by exploring the scientific literature, by conducting interviews with relevant parties and by relying on observations. The following six key questions must be answered in order to establish a problem definition.

1. What is the problem?
Describe the problem in as much detail as possible by asking various specific questions about the nature of the problem.

2. Why is it a problem?
Describe the consequences of the problem in detail and make clear to what extent each of those is perceived to be a problem. Since when is it a problem? Describe the historical background of the problem. When did it first emerge and when was it first noticed? Has the severity of the problem increased or decreased over time?

3. For whom is it a problem?
Describe all the parties that are involved in the problem, both in terms of who causes the problem, who suffers from the problem, and who is responsible for tackling the problem. Describe the different perspectives that each of these parties has on the problem and whether these are compatible or not. Also, describe whether the problem definition needs to be adjusted in order to incorporate the different takes on the problem.

4. What are the possible causes of the problem?
Describe the possible causes and background of the problem. What might cause it and what could explain the emergence of the problem? Use the double question: What causes the problem and how do these causes affect the problem?

5. What is/are the target group(s)?
Describe the actors or groups that a possible intervention should be targeted at. Whom should be convinced of the problem? Whose cooperation is necessary for the problem to be solved?

6. What are the key aspects of the problem?
Describe whether it is an applied problem that you are dealing with and whether it is a concrete problem. In addition, describe the social psychological aspects to the problem and give an indication of whether the problem can be tackled or solved through social psychological intervention.

SUGGESTED FURTHER READING

Schaalma, H.P., Kok, G., Bosker, R.J. & Parcel, G.S. (1996). Planned development and evaluation of AIDS/STD education for secondary school students in the Netherlands: Short-term effects. *Health Education Quarterly*, *23(4)*, 469–487.

Semin, G. R. & Fielder, K. (1996). *Applied Social Psychology*. London: Sage. (This book contains many interesting applied research programmes from Europe.)

Stern, P. C. (2000). New environmental theories: Toward a coherent theory of environmentally significant behavior. *Journal of Social Issues*, *56(3)*, 407–424.

ASSIGNMENT 2

The manager of a university hospital asks you, as a social psychologist, for advice. According to the manager the burn-out rate among the nurses is unacceptably high and, worse, it is still rising. Last year about 10 per cent of all nurses called in sick with symptoms of burn-out. Two years ago this was only 5 per cent. Like a virus, the burn-out seems to be spreading throughout the hospital: departments that used to have very low absenteeism, now report high numbers of burned-out nurses. In addition, patients have started complaining about the hastiness and bad temper of the nurses, about receiving too little attention and being physically cared for insufficiently. According to the manager, the nurses are simply not very motivated and should be dealt with firmly. The nurses, however, complain about the workload that has increased ever since the reorganization of the hospital that took place two years previously.

(a) What is the problem exactly and why? Conduct imaginary interviews with the manager of the hospital plus some nurses (both healthy and those on sick leave) and patients to clarify the problem.
(b) What are the possible causes of the problem?

  - How could the problem have started? Give preliminary explanations for the problem.
  - What may be the causes of the problem and by what processes might these causes generate the problem?

To generate ideas about possible causes and explanations, read:

Bakker, A.B. & Schaufeli, W.B. (2000). Burnout contagion processes among teachers. *Journal of Applied Social Psychology, 30(11)*, 2289–2308.
Le Blanc, P.M., Bakker, A.B., Peeters, M.C.W., Maria C. W., Van Heesch, N. C. A. & Schaufeli, W.B. (2001). Emotional job demands and burnout among oncology care providers. *Anxiety, Stress & Coping: An International Journal, 14(3)*, 243–263.

Verbeke, W (1997). Individual differences in **emotional contagion** of salespersons: Its effect on performance and burnout. *Psychology & Marketing, 14(6)*, 617–636.

(c) To what extent is the problem an applied, concrete and social psychological problem and why? What attitudes, affective responses, or behaviour play a role in the problem? To what extent are other types of explanations and interventions relevant?
(d) Can the problem be solved or relieved? What should be the target group(s) of the social psychological intervention? To what extent are those involved motivated to solve the problem?
(e) Use the information you have gathered and the questions in Box 2.4 to formulate an adequate problem definition.

CHAPTER 3

THE ANALYSIS PHASE: FINDING THEORY-BASED EXPLANATIONS FOR PROBLEMS

Contents

The Analysis Phase: Finding Theory-based Explanations for Problems

INTRODUCTION

In the Problem phase (Chapter 2) we have already explored some possible explanations for the problem. In the Analysis phase we continue the search for explanations. First, we define the *outcome variable,* that is, the variable that we want to change. Ideally the outcome variable should be phrased in terms of the desired end situation (for example, tolerance towards ethnic police officers). Subsequently, in the *divergent* stage we try to generate as many explanations as possible and try to link these explanations to relevant social psychological theories. Finally, in the *convergent* stage we evaluate each of the theory-based explanations in terms of their relevance, validity, and plausibility for the problem under investigation.

SPECIFYING THE OUTCOME VARIABLE

What do we want to influence? In the previous chapter we stated that the problem must be operationalized as precisely as possible, specifying exactly what the problem is, why and for whom it is a problem, and the main causes of the problem. After formulating a problem definition it is often clear what variable we want to explain, and eventually change to remedy the problem. For example, in tackling workplace bullying it is quite clear that bullying is the problem and that interventions should focus on dealing with bullying tactics (Smith, Talamelli, Cowie, Naylor & Chauhan, 2004). Thus, the outcome variable here – what must be explained and changed – is bullying behaviour. Yet the outcome variable has not always been properly identified in the Problem phase. A first aim of the Analysis phase is to specify the outcome variable or variables in order to clarify what the target behaviours are for intervention. In our case, that variable often has a social psychological dimension. As stated before, ideally the outcome variable will be phrased in terms of the desired end state, for example, less bullying in the workplace, more garbage recycling, a reduction in teenage pregnancies, more positive attitudes toward gays.

By and large, the literature distinguishes between three different social psychological variables (see for example, Aronson, Wilson & Akert, 2002; Brehm, Kassin & Fein, 2005; Hewstone, Stroebe & Jonas, 2005; Hogg & Vaughan, 2005; Kenrick, Neuberg & Cialdini, 2005; Myers, 2005).

1. *Behaviours and behavioural intentions*: how do we (intend to) behave? Examples are aggression, absenteeism, anti-social behaviour, sexism, smoking, dieting, donating to charity, and volunteering.
2. *Attitudes and cognitions*: what do we think and value? Examples are attitudes towards ethnic minority members, beliefs and optimism about personal health, knowledge about safe sex practices, preferences for modes of transport, support for abortion programmes.
3. *Emotions or affect*: what do we feel? Examples are fear of death, anger towards authorities, stress feelings, feelings about unfairness at work, worries about one's unhealthy practices, but also positive feelings like joy, happiness, and sympathy.

Sometimes an explanatory model incorporates behavioural, attitudinal as well as emotional factors, for example, in research programmes about smoking and dieting (Kok et al., 1996). As another example, in a study on absenteeism, Geurts, Buunk and Schaufeli (1994) examined how feelings of resentment and perceptions of one's own work situation relative to others predicted absenteeism.

With any problem it is vital for applied social psychologists to determine as early as possible what their primary outcome variable will be. Frequently the problem is defined only at a macro-level, for example, environmental pollution, gun crime or the incidence of breast cancer. In many cases, such societal problems are the starting point for research and intervention. For example, policy makers generally will be concerned about an increase in gun or knife killings, the air pollution in main industrial areas, or the number of women dying of breast cancer. However, social psychologists can affect these problems only indirectly, through inducing changes in a specific set of behaviours, attitudes, and feelings in a specific set of individuals. For example, pollution can be reduced if more people ride bikes instead of driving cars (Van Vugt et al., 1995). Gun crime can be tackled by making it more difficult for people to buy guns (Podell & Archer, 1994). The incidence of breast cancer can be reduced if women regularly engage in breast self-examination. Biking to work, a decreased interest in guns, and engaging in breast self-examination are the sort of outcome variables which are of interest to applied scientists using the PATH model.

It is preferable in the first instance to focus on a single outcome variable rather than a set of variables. First, the variables might be so closely related that a change in one factor will automatically produce a change in the other. In the context of healthy eating, for example, attitudes and behaviours are often related (Brug, Oenema & Campbell, 2003). Thus, it is assumed that a change in preference towards healthy food increases the sales of healthy foods like fruit and vegetables. Therefore, it is not necessary to include both variables as outcome variables: focusing on 'a preference for healthy food' as the outcome variable will suffice.

Second, when outcome variables are not directly related, it is often because they have a different ontogenetic history, and therefore require quite different explanations and interventions. For example, there are generally weak correlations between a range of environmentally relevant behaviours like recycling, energy use, water conservation, and transportation (Gardner & Stern, 1996; Schulz & Oskamp, 2000). Hence, explanations for garbage recycling may have little to do with accounts of why people use buses or conserve energy or water. Accordingly, it would be unwise to incorporate them into a single PATH model. It is therefore clear that social psychologists must be selective in their decisions on what to focus on and choose between several outcome variables.

Box 3.1   Interview with Professor Dieter Frey of the University of Munich (Germany)

'I first got interested in applied social psychology more than 25 years ago. I began my applied research with a series of studies on the recuperation process after severe accidents and surgeries. I applied the basic social psychology of control theory and helplessness theory to this area. Our research showed that the recuperation process after severe accidents in large part depends on the answers to the following questions:

- Are victims asking the 'Why me?' question ('Why did this happen to me?')?
- Do they think the accident could have been avoided?
- Do they think they were responsible for the accident?
- Can they foresee the process of recuperation?
- Do they think they can control the recuperation?

We found that the people who recover best are those who do not ask the 'Why me?' question, who see the accident as unavoidable, who do not hold themselves responsible for the accident, who can foresee the process of recuperation and who think that they can influence the recuperation process. Hopefully, this research contributed to a better understanding of the aftermath of severe accidents and to a better way of coping with such life crises for victims, their families and the social workers working with them.

'Later in my career, I did applied research on the environment and in the organizational field. In particular, I got more interested in how our social psychological theories can be applied in the natural setting of processes of motivation, leadership, optimizing teamwork, and innovation. For the future, I am very optimistic about applied social psychological research. I think that we will see an increase in research and the application of our knowledge, especially with regard to problems such as an ageing population and the needs of elderly people. I am glad about this development. In my opinion basic research alone is too boring (at least for me). Apart from this we have fascinating ideas in basic research that can be excellently applied in natural settings. It would be a waste not to do so.'

Interested in Dieter Frey's work? Then read, for instance:

Frey, D. (1985). Psychological determinants in the convalescence of accident patients. *Basic and Applied Social Psychology, 6(4)*, 317–328.
Frey, D. & Brodbeck, F. (2002). Group processes in organizations. In N.J. Smelser & P. Baltes (Eds.), *International Encyclopedia of Social and Behavioral Sciences* (*Band 9*, pp. 6407–6413). Amsterdam, the Netherlands: Elsevier Science.

REQUIREMENTS FOR THE OUTCOME VARIABLE

In order to be a useful target of influence, an outcome variable must meet the following criteria:

1. it must be relevant to the problem (*relevance*);
2. it must be described in specific and concrete terms (s*pecificity*);
3. it must be described in continuous terms (*continuity*).

Relevance

The outcome variable must be relevant to the problem. First, the outcome variable must follow on logically from the problem definition. If the problem analysis suggests, for example, that there is a high turnover among ethnic officers in the police force, then it would make sense to choose as the outcome variable a reduction in the turnover of ethnic officers rather than recruiting more ethnic minority staff. Or, in efforts to promote volunteering activities to help the aged, the outcome variable should be the willingness of people to do volunteer work rather than improving the welfare of the people that are being helped, which is, of course, the ultimate goal. Thus, the outcome variable must closely follow the problem definition and should ideally reflect the desired state (for example, less turnover, more energy conservation).

Specificity

The variable must be described in specific, concrete terms. In the PATH model, the outcome variable ought to be as concrete as possible. Rather than talking about a need to discourage anti-social behaviours in general, one should target a particular activity. For instance, one should focus instead on concrete behaviours like littering, vandalism, graffiti, and so on. Even something like 'household recycling' may not be specific enough for an intervention, and one might need to focus instead on recycling garden waste in particular. Specifying the outcome variable is important because outcome variables that are formulated too broadly make it hard to develop an intervention programme that effectively deals with the problem. An intervention programme based on an outcome variable that is defined too broadly, runs the risk of influencing aspects of the outcome variable that are not problematic at all while they may leave intact the aspect that is. For instance, when the government wants to encourage citizens to recycle paper, an information campaign developed to affect citizens' 'household recycling' (outcome variable) may affect the recycling of glass (which is not the problem) but not the recycling of paper. Thus, social psychologists must be very specific about which variables they wish to focus on.

Continuity

The variable must be continuous so that it can be described in quantitative terms ('less' or 'more'). It is useful to describe the outcome variable in quantitative terms, for example, in terms of frequency ('How often do you go to work by car?') or intensity ('How much do you enjoy smoking?'). Factors such as 'recruitment policy' or 'choice of travel mode' are inadequate as outcome variables because they cannot be described in terms of 'more' or 'less'. There are two reasons why it is important to choose a continuous outcome variable. First, it makes it easier to generate explanations for the problem, and describe the causal model. For example, one can think of specific explanations for why some people use their car more frequently than others, or why people enjoy exercise more or less. In contrast, finding a satisfactory explanation for an insufficiently quantified outcome variable such as 'choice of travel mode' is almost impossible, because it is unclear what aspect of the outcome variable one aims to influence and how. For instance, does one want to convince travellers to choose a *different kind* of travel mode from the car, or suggest they travel *more frequently* by train?

Second, a quantifiable variable helps in evaluating the success of an intervention programme. If interventions to promote fitness and exercise are successful then people should report that they exercise more frequently after the intervention. If an intervention to decrease littering in a neighbourhood is effective this means there should be less litter on the streets after the intervention. In contrast, if an outcome variable cannot be described in quantitative terms, the social psychologist or policy maker will not be able to measure and evaluate the effectiveness of the intervention so easily. The result is that no-one will know for sure whether the intervention has helped or not. For example, it is impossible to evaluate an intervention aimed at influencing the outcome variable 'ethnic recruitment policy', simply because it is not possible to measure the variable 'recruitment policy' in a quantitative way.

We appreciate that it is not always possible to come up with a quantification of the outcome variable. For obvious reasons, health professionals might be more interested in *whether or not* teenagers smoke rather than *how much* they smoke a day. In that case, their outcome variable is binary (namely, smoker vs. non-smoker) and the success of an intervention is measured in terms of the number or percentage of teenagers who give up smoking.

THE DIVERGENT PHASE: GENERATING EXPLANATIONS

After specifying the outcome variable, the second task in the Analysis phase is to try to generate as many explanations as possible and identify the relevant causes of the problem. This is the *divergent* phase. There are a number of things to consider in this phase.

First, the scientific validity of the explanations matters less at this stage. It is more important to be exhaustive to ensure important factors are not being omitted from the analysis at this point. Second, in this stage the social psychologist should focus on possible explanations for *differences* in the outcome variable. If the outcome variable is condom use among youngsters, focus on why youngsters might or might not use condoms, rather than on why they have sex with strangers or act irresponsibly in terms of their sexual behaviour.

There are various methods available to help social psychologists generate a list of explanations. First, free association techniques can be used to look at a problem, creatively examining it from many different angles. Explanations can also be derived from empirical techniques such as surveys, interviews or observations. Third, one could examine the social psychological literature to find explanations.

Free Association

To use an association technique for generating explanations, it is important not to be overly critical and selective in the first instance. Much like brainstorming techniques (see Brodbeck & Greitemeyer, 2000; Paulus & Dzindolet, 1993), it is best to first generate many explanations. This is followed by a more systematic analysis, which looks into the validity of each explanation and selects the more promising ones for further inquiry. Furthermore, free association can lead from one explanation to another, possibly better, explanation. In explaining why young male drivers are more likely to be involved in traffic accidents, a social psychologist might initially conclude that these drivers simply do not have the money to buy a new and safer car, until one realizes that this then should also apply to young female drivers. Yet female drivers are much less accident prone (Elander, West & French, 1993). This leads to a new explanation that young males take more risks when they are driving, and are therefore more likely to be involved in traffic accidents (which is true, just ask the car insurance industry). Thus, building on other ideas via association can be fruitful.

We should distinguish between different association techniques, *problem association, concept association*, and *perspective taking*.

1. *Problem association*

The most straightforward form of association is to start with the problem itself, for example, traffic accidents caused by young male drivers. The social psychologist could begin with generating five or more explanations for the problem by asking himself why the problem is a problem. Again, it does not matter at this stage whether the explanations are valid or not. For example, the social psychologist could come up with the following explanations:

- Young men cannot afford to buy safe cars.
- Young men are worse drivers.
- Young men take more risks while driving their car.
- Young men believe they get more status from their peers by driving riskily.
- Young male drivers think they are less likely to be involved in an accident or suffer death or injury.

By adopting a problem-focused approach, the social psychologist generates a number of promising explanations which could be looked at more closely using the scientific literature. There is a risk, however, in focusing too narrowly on the problem – accident proneness among young male drivers – while ignoring other relevant explanations. Therefore, it is also important to search for explanations through a conceptual and more abstract approach.

2. *Concept association*

Another way to generate explanations is to move beyond the problem and look for phenomena that might be conceptually similar to the problem under investigation. For example, car accidents among young male drivers can be viewed in terms of risk-taking which poses the question whether young men are generally more risk-taking (which they are; see, for example, Daly & Wilson, 2001). Similarly, male driving behaviour could be looked at by invoking explanations based on status (driving riskily gives more status), optimism (young men are too optimistic about the risks of fast driving), responsibility (young men have a lack of responsibility), and social norms (norms in their peer group encourage risky driving). By introducing these concepts, the social psychologist has translated the problem into a more abstract, scientific problem, which facilitates further analysis.

As another example, if one wants to explain why smiling waiters receive more tips (Van Baaren, Holland, Steenaert & Van Knippenberg, 2003), one could, among others, focus on concepts such as sympathy (people give more to others they like), positive mood (seeing another person smile enhances one's mood), and exchange (people feel more obliged to give a tip to someone who has just 'given' them a smile). Each of these concepts can then be used to formulate a preliminary explanatory model which can be tested in subsequent research.

3. *Perspective taking*

Perspective taking might also be useful as an association technique. Here one looks at the problem through the eyes of different actors. First, one defines which individuals are possibly involved in the problem, and next one puts oneself in the shoes of each of them. For example, do young male drivers actually perceive that they take more risks than others? How would I feel about myself as a young man when I drove very carefully? How would women view risky or careful drivers? How would I react to an unfriendly waiter? What type of feeling does it give me when someone smiles at me? How would I feel as an ethnic minority member in an overwhelmingly white police force? How would I feel if ethnic minority people were my colleagues? Various concepts might be invoked through perspective-taking techniques, which could be useful in generating explanations. For instance, imagine yourself as a young man with a car – you may come up with such concepts as 'adventure', 'excitement', 'adrenaline', or 'girls', which offer potentially useful avenues for further inquiry.

Interviews and Observations

We suggested that interviews and observations could be useful tools in the Problem stage (Chapter 2) when it is important to find out more about the problem. Interview and observation techniques are also useful in the Analysis phase when social psychologists must generate explanations. Here interviews and observations are of a slightly different nature than in the Problem phase, because they are conducted in light of the chosen outcome variables (for example, giving up smoking, donating money for victims of HIV/AIDS, degree of tolerance towards ethnic police officers). Hence, they will be more specific than in the previous stage.

For example, suppose a social psychologist is asked by a large company to examine why so few women in that company are being promoted to higher level management functions. While interviewing female employees to formulate the problem (see Chapter 2), he discovers that many of them are simply not attracted to a job in management. He therefore defines as the outcome variable the lack of interest among women in management positions. As part of the Analysis phase, the next wave of interviews could focus on why there is a lack of interest in these jobs among women. Perhaps he finds that many women believe they cannot really do the job well or that they lack support from male managers (Lyness & Thompson, 2000). In addition, the social psychologist might decide to sit in at various job interviews to observe the interactions between men and women in the company.

1. *Interviews*

A specific interview tool to help generate explanations is the 'why interview'. This could be a genuine interview with relevant parties, but it could also be an imaginary exercise to force the social psychologist to think about potential causes for the problem. Such interviews are very suitable to look at the processes underlying the problem, and are therefore more detailed than the exploratory interviews that we discussed in the Problem phase (Chapter 2). It is important in these interviews to consider which outcome variables must ultimately be influenced through intervention.

With social psychological problems, the most likely questions concern why people behave the way they behave, and why they think or feel the way they do. It is important in such interviews to vary the questions. Constantly repeating the 'why' question might annoy the interviewees, and such questions might put them on the defensive. Instead, try asking questions like 'What makes you think that?', 'What is it about that that … ', 'Why do you think that?', that might be more fruitful. Here is an example of a social psychologist interviewing a female employee who has refused to accept a management position at her company:

> *Female employee:* 'I didn't want the job.'
> *Social psychologist:* 'Why not?'
> *Female employee:* 'I didn't feel it was the right job for me.'

Social psychologist:	'Why wasn't it right for you?'
Female employee:	'I don't like to tell other people what to do.'
Social psychologist:	'What is it about that that you don't like?'
Female employee:	'I don't think they would listen to me.'
Social psychologist:	'Why do you think that?'
Female employee:	'Maybe because most of them are men and they don't take women managers very seriously.'
Social psychologist:	'What makes you think that? Can you give examples?'
Female employee:	'There haven't been any female managers and the one who was briefly here left the job after less than a year.'
Social psychologist:	'Why do you think that is?'
Female employee:	'Because she couldn't get along with her staff.'
Social psychologist:	'What type of problems did she have with the staff?'
Female employee:	'Her staff thought that the only reason she got the job was because of an affirmative action programme.'
Social psychologist:	'And was this true, do you think?'
Female employee:	'No, but I don't think the top management in the company did enough to support her.'
Social psychologist:	'What makes you think that?'
Female employee:	'Hm ... maybe they thought that helping her would give out the wrong signal.'
Social psychologist:	'What kind of wrong signal?'
Female employee:	'Perhaps they were afraid that it would undermine her authority if they offered help.'

Admittedly, the questions posed by the social psychologist are a bit unimaginative. But the example shows that by systematically asking a series of 'why' type questions, the social psychologist gets a feeling for the underlying processes that might explain why women are not so keen to take on management jobs in this particular company. Through the interview, a picture emerges in which the lack of interest in management positions among women might have something to do with the (lack of) support they get from subordinates and superiors in the company. This might be reinforced by the affirmative action programme within the company that sends out the wrong message about the quality of female managers.

We can present this explanatory model in a figure (see Figure 3.1), whereby we move back in the causal chain, bottom-up, from the outcome variable (the lack of interest among women in management positions) to a potential obstacle for achieving this (the performance expectations of female managers as influenced by affirmative action plans).

This model is by no means complete and it raises many new *why* questions. For example, what is the relationship between affirmative action policies and the performance expectations of female managers? Do different departments respond differently to female managers, for example, depending upon whether they are male or female dominated? Are there other reasons why women are not interested in taking up management positions in the company? These questions might lead to a whole set of new explanations, which could be captured in a process model like the one in Figure 3.1. At this stage it is important to be exhaustive, so one should not yet focus too much on one set of explanations, for example, the low performance expectations of female managers.

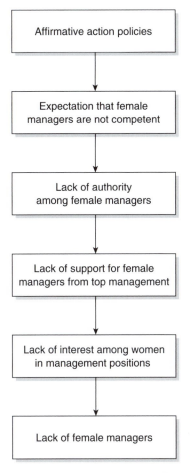

Figure 3.1   A Process Model to Explain the Deficiency of Female Managers

Cutting down the number of explanations and concentrating on the most relevant ones is something that will not happen until the convergent phase.

2. Observations

Observational data are also useful for generating explanations. In the Problem phase (Chapter 2), observations were unsystematic. They were used to get a better understanding of the problem. Observational research in the Analysis phase is more structured and social psychologists may use standard observation instruments in order to illuminate the causes and consequences of a particular social problem. We can distinguish between the observations of others and self-observation (introspection).

In the case of observation the social psychologists and/or their assistants observe a process in a group or organization. Take, for example, a social psychologist who has been asked to aid a large hospital in solving decision-making problems in a management team which is concerned with patient waiting lists. Some team members have complained about the poor decision-making processes and the constant conflicts between representatives of the hospital management and medical staff. After several interviews with key members of the staff, the social psychologist defines the problem in terms of trying to improve the consensus and decision-making quality in this team with regard to the waiting lists for patients. He now wants to find out why there are problems in the decision-making processes and decides to systematically observe the team meetings.

He uses SYMLOG, a group observation instrument (Bales & Cohen, 1979), which he is trained in. The SYMLOG instrument consists of 26 ratings that are given to each group member. (The full list of items is displayed in Box 3.2.) Examples are items such as 'Active, dominant, talks a lot', 'Unfriendly, negativistic', and 'Analytical, task oriented, problem solving' that the social psychologist has to score on a three-point scale (1 = rarely, 2 = sometimes, 3 = often). These 26 categories are then combined to yield scores for each team member on three main dimensions: (a) dominant–submissive, (b) friendly–unfriendly, (c) instrumentally controlled–emotionally expressive. With these data observers can create a graphic representation of a group.

For example, SYMLOG could reveal that one or two members are clearly dominating the team discussion. Furthermore, the analysis might reveal that there is a conflict between more analytical and more emotional team members. This might help the social psychologist to understand the poor quality of team decision making.

Box 3.2 The Items of the SYMLOG Group Observation Instrument

1. Active, dominant, talks a lot.
2. Extroverted, outgoing, positive.
3. A purposeful, democratic task leader.
4. An assertive business-like leader.
5. Authoritarian, controlling, disapproving.
6. Domineering, tough-minded, powerful.
7. Provocative, egocentric, shows off.
8. Jokes around, expressive, dramatic.
9. Entertaining, sociable, smiling, warm.
10. Friendly, equalitarian.
11. Works cooperatively with others.
12. Analytical, task-oriented, problem solving.
13. Legalistic, has to be right.
14. Unfriendly, negativistic.
15. Irritable, cynical, won't cooperate.
16. Shows feelings and emotions.
17. Affectionate, likeable, fun to be with.

18. Looks up to others, appreciative, trustful.
19. Gentle, willing to accept responsibility.
20. Obedient, works submissively.
21. Self-punishing, works too hard.
22. Depressed, sad, resentful, rejecting.
23. Alienated, quits, withdraws.
24. Afraid to try, doubts own ability.
25. Quietly happy just to be with others.
26. Passive, introverted, says little.

In the case of introspective methods people are enabled to examine their own behaviour within a certain time interval. Rather than through external, expert observation, the social psychologist might ask the actors to rate themselves as they interact with others. One of the authors of this book used this technique in a study among police officers (Buunk & Verhoeven, 1991). This research examined the causes of stress among police officers in the Netherlands. Each working day within a five day period, officers were asked to write down every stressful experience they had using a diary method. The researchers were able to distinguish between five stress categories based on these self-observations:

1. emergency situations, for example, a serious car accident;
2. collaboration problems with other officers, for example, about the share of duties;
3. conflicts with the public, for example, in making arrests;
4. work overload, for example, in doing administration;
5. work underload, for example, a night shift without much work to do.

Because each stress incident was described in detail, it was possible to create a rich database of different stressors. The researchers then focused on the greatest stressors among police officers. Interestingly, the most stressful category was collaboration with colleagues. Hence, the process model and the subsequent intervention plan focused on this particular stressor. This example shows how a carefully conducted diary study can help explain a particular problem and set up an intervention plan.

Social Psychological Theories

A third method for generating explanations is through the use of the social psychological literature. Social psychological theories, which are usually based on a large number of studies, specify the potential causes underlying social behaviours as diverse as aggression, altruism, leadership, status, conformity and prejudice. For example, bystander intervention theory (Fischer, Greitemeyer, Pollozek & Frey, 2006; Latané & Darley, 1970) explains why people often fail to assist people in an emergency like a road accident. Researchers observed that some people are reluctant to help because they don't know exactly how to help or don't feel personally responsible. When a social psychologist is asked to develop an educational campaign to promote emergency helping, he could use this theory to generate explanations for why such helping is not more widespread. There are many other social psychological theories and they each focus on a specific social phenomenon or behaviour. A list of the major theories, phenomena, and concepts in social psychology is given in the Glossary which includes a short description of each. A more complete list can be found in any major text in social psychology.

The two methods for generating explanations – association and perspective taking – will often give a clue as to what social psychological theories are relevant. For example, bullying can be seen as a form of aggression (free association) that may be triggered by an incident that lowers the bully's self-esteem, such as receiving criticism or a low grade (perspective taking). This suggests that a social psychologist should look into the literature on aggression and self-esteem for possible explanations. Likewise, an unhealthy diet may be seen as a bad habit (free association), but might also be a way to deal with relationship stress (perspective taking). In that case, a social psychologist should look into the literature on learning, automatic behaviours, and relationship problems for possible explanations. Note that in the Analysis phase, these theories are still

KT primarily used for **heuristic** purposes to develop an exploratory causal model. In the next stage of the PATH model, the Test phase (Chapter 4), each of these theories will be considered in depth.

There are three different strategies to use from the social psychological literature for generating explanations, namely the topical strategy, the conceptual strategy, and the general theory strategy.

1. The topical strategy

This approach finds out what is written in the literature on this particular topic. In many cases, there are studies in the psychological literature that will be directly relevant for the problem. For example, if absenteeism in the workplace is the problem of interest, a social psychologist can try to find out what has been published about absenteeism in the workplace in the social, industrial, and organizational literatures. He might find, for example, that perceptions of conflict between work and family are an important cause of job absenteeism, especially among women (Boyar, Maertz & Pearson, 2005). As another example, if smoking cessation is the outcome variable, then the social psychol-

KT ogist will discover that there are numerous studies that examine factors involved in stopping smoking, and that **social support** from peers plays an important role (DiClemente, Prochaska, Fairhurst and Velicer, 1991).

2. Conceptual strategy

This approach reformulates the problem on a conceptually higher level to find links with relevant social psychological phenomena and theories (see the Glossary). For example, absenteeism can be seen as a stress response, which might encourage the social

psychologist to look into stress theories (Folkman, Lazarus, Donkel-Schetter, DcLongis & $\boxed{\text{KT}}$
Gruen, 2000). Absenteeism may also be regarded as a form of free-riding in which
people do not pull their weight for the organization they work for (Cooper, Dyck & $\boxed{\text{KT}}$
Frohlich, 1992; Koslowsky & Krausz, 2002). This leads the social psychologist to look into
the literature on **social loafing** (Karau & Williams, 1993), **social dilemmas** (Kerr & Tindale, $\boxed{\text{KT}}$
2004; Van Vugt & Samuelson, 2001), and **diffusion of responsibility** (Latané & Darley,
1970). Absenteeism might be caused by feelings of unfair treatment by management, which $\boxed{\text{KT}}$
suggests a link with the literature about **distributive** and **procedural fairness** (Geurts, $\boxed{\text{KT}}$
Schaufeli & Buunk, 1993; Lind & Tyler, 1997), or absenteeism might be explained as a lack
of identification with the organization, suggesting the relevance of applying concepts from $\boxed{\text{KT}}$
social identity theory (Abrams & Hogg, 2004) or **self-categorization theory** (Hogg &
Turner, 1987). $\boxed{\text{KT}}$

3. General theory strategy

The topical and conceptual approaches can be characterized as inductive in that one moves
'bottom-up', from problem to explanation. The general theory strategy is deductive. It
moves 'top-down', from a generic theory that at first sight may not seem directly relevant
for the problem to potential explanations. Such general theories about human behaviour (see
the Glossary) include attitude-behaviour theories (Ajzen, 1991; Ajzen & Fishbein, 2000),
social exchange theories (Thibaut & Kelley, 1959), learning theories (Bandura, 1986;
Skinner, 1956), cultural theories (Markus & Kitayama, 2003), and **evolutionary psychology** $\boxed{\text{KT}}$
theories (Schaller, Simpson & Kenrick, 2006; Van Vugt, 2006).

It is not always immediately clear what these theories contribute to understanding the
social problem, but they have a wide range of implications across a broad domain of
problems and especially when it is difficult to use a topical or conceptual strategy, for
example, because the focal problem is relatively new (for example, attitudes toward
genetically modified food or a new disease), a general theory search might be very
helpful. Furthermore, these general theories are often easy to find in textbooks on social
psychology. Most social psychologists have their 'favourite' theories which they apply
to a range of social psychological problems. For example, an evolutionary social
psychologist might view absenteeism as a flight response to a potentially threatening
situation. A cultural social psychologist may interpret it as resulting from a 'culture of
absence' in which it is normal or even encouraged to be absent from work. An exchange
social psychologist might view this behaviour in terms of a mismatch between what
people put into the organization and what they get out of it.

In the Glossary we present an overview of the main social psychological theories.
This list gives a global idea of the literature, but is by no means exhaustive. For further
information about social psychological theories, we would refer to introductory textbooks on social psychology (for example, Aronson, Wilson & Akert, 2005; Brehm
et al., 2005; Hewstone, Stroebe & Jonas, 2005; Kenrick et al., 2005; Meyers, 2005).
We particularly recommend *The Blackwell Encyclopedia of Social Psychology,* edited
by Manstead and Hewstone (1995), which provides a concise summary of all major
theories and concepts in social psychology.

THEORETICAL APPROACHES UNDER INVESTIGATION: THE CASE OF SAFE SEX PROMOTION

We illustrate the divergent phase of the Analysis step by means of a case about sexually transmitted diseases (STDs). We will start our case with the problem and its definition (the Problem phase; see Chapter 2). Health education authorities have noted a sharp rise in the prevalence of STDs particularly among teenagers. Research has found that this problem is largely due to an increase in unsafe sex practices, especially among teenagers and where they have sex without using condoms. In combination with the very real threats of contracting HIV/AIDS and unwanted pregnancy, they decide to ask a team of social psychologists to develop interventions to promote safe sex practices among schools (this example is adapted from Kok et al., 1996).

The social psychologists first develop a problem definition, which is stated as follows:

> There is an increase in the prevalence of STDs among teenagers in Britain, which poses various serious health risks (such as infections leading to infertility) for people who have an STD and those who have sexual contact with them. STDs are costly to treat and impose a burden on the budgets of clinics and hospitals. STDs can be influenced by the promotion of safe-sex practices, in particular the use of condoms. This programme aims to increase the knowledge about condom use in relation to STDs and increase condom use.

Thus, the social psychologists initially focus on outcome variables that are cognitive (knowledge about STDs) and behavioural (using condoms).

Box 3.3   A Case Study: Feedback to Eyewitnesses' Identification of a Suspect

Imagine the following situation.

> An eyewitness, Sarah, is asked to identify her attacker on viewing a line-up: 'Oh, my God, … I don't know … It's one of those two but I don't know which one.' Thirty minutes later Sarah is still viewing the line-up and having difficulty making a decision: 'I don't know … number two?'. The officer administering the line-up says: 'Okay, you identified the subject', and writes down number two. Three months later, at the trial, the judge asks Sarah: 'You were positive that, at the line-up, it was number two? It wasn't a maybe?'. Sarah: 'There was no maybe about it, I was absolutely positive.'

A false identification may have enormous consequences. In the case of wrongful imprisonment the innocent person is punished for a crime he/she did not commit, while the real criminal is still on the loose and may strike again. In addition, the government and taxpayer suffer financially: one year of imprisonment costs about 33,000

---

dollars per prisoner. In general, judges and/or jurors value a witness testimony more, as the eyewitness is more certain of his/her identification. There is, however, only a very modest relation between eyewitness confidence and eyewitness accuracy.

Psychologists Wells and Bradfield* from the Iowa State University examined a potentially important factor that may affect eye witness certainty, namely feedback from a police officer following identification in a line-up. In their experiment participants viewed a security video in which a gunman walked in front of the camera. Participants were subsequently asked to identify the gunman from a photo-spread. The actual gunman was, however, not in the photo-spread and all of the eyewitnesses made false identifications. Following the identification, witnesses were given confirming feedback ('Good, you identified the actual suspect in the case'), disconfirming feedback ('Oh. You identified X. Actually, the suspect is Y'), or no feedback. Participants were then asked questions about the video and to give a written description of the gunman.

Compared to participants who had received no feedback, participants who had received disconfirming feedback reported less certainty about the identification, having had a lower clarity of memory and a worse view, and estimated they needed more time to arrive at an identification. On the contrary, despite the fact that they had made false identifications as well, participants who had received confirming feedback reported more certainty about the identification, having had a better view and a higher clarity of **memory**, and estimated they needed less time to arrive at an identification. On the basis of their study, Wells and Bradfield strongly recommend that the police officer who administers the line-up or photo-spread should be someone who does not know which person is the real suspect and that he/she should secure a confidence statement from the eyewitness *at the time* of the identification.

KT

*Wells, G.L. & Bradfield, A.L. (1998). 'Good, you identified the suspect': Feedback to eyewitnesses distorts their reports of the witnessing experience. *Journal of Applied Psychology, 83(3),* 360–376.

A Topical Strategy

In generating theory-based explanations for the problem of STDs and condom use failure, the most straightforward approach is to find examples in the literature of research programmes on STDs and condom use. There might not be much on condom use in relation to STDs, but there is presumably a lot of research on determinants of condom use, for example, in relation to HIV/AIDS and pregnancy. Searches on PsycINFO, the electronic database for the psychological literature, reveal no fewer than 2075 hits with 'condom use' as key words and 1512 with 'STD' as a key word (at the time of writing). The combination of 'condom use and STD' reveals a more manageable number of 312 hits, and their abstracts can be inspected in terms of their relevance for this problem. Articles that review a large part of the literature – so-called 'reviews' and 'meta-analyses' – are particularly useful. This literature might reveal a number of interesting conclusions which could be used to generate explanations for why teenagers fail to use condoms in relation to STDs. For example:

- Condom use in relation to avoiding STDs is regarded by teenagers as a sensible strategy.
- Most teenagers believe they have a less than average risk of contracting an STD.
- Condom use is regarded as unpleasant, particularly among sexually active teenagers.
- Condom use among peers is not perceived to be widespread by teenagers.
- Some teenagers are embarrassed to purchase condoms or go to their doctor for help.
- Teenagers report difficulties with carrying a condom around.
- Teenagers find it difficult to negotiate condom use with a sexual partner.

It is generally recommended to start with a topical approach, first, because it allows social psychologists to use the knowledge of previous research to distinguish between likely and unlikely explanations for problems. For example, research shows that most teenagers perceive condom use as a sensible strategy. This suggests that knowledge about the benefits of condom use is perhaps not the main obstacle, which could help social psychologists in developing a process model. The second reason why it is recommended to begin with this strategy is that one immediately obtains a valid insight into a problem. Indeed, if several studies show that knowledge about the benefits of condom use is widespread among teenagers then social psychologists may safely assume that this is the case. A third advantage is that often there will be examples of intervention programmes reported in the literature. This enables social psychologists to make a judgement at an early stage about the intervention potential of particular explanations.

There are also disadvantages with this approach. First, the generalization of the research might be a problem. Suppose most of the research on condom use has been done in Western Europe. One cannot simply assume that the same findings will also be found among teenage populations in North America or Africa. Second, there is always a risk of changing the problem into one that is already in the literature. By doing this, social psychologists could lose sight of the specific problem that they were asked to investigate. For example, research might suggest that teenagers are more likely to use condoms to avoid pregnancy. Yet the social psychologists were being asked to examine strategies to foster condom use in relation to the threat of STDs. A third problem is that by looking in detail at other programmes, social psychologists could become a bit complacent and not think actively and creatively about a problem. There is, for example, the risk of uncritically adopting programmes that are not properly evaluated or do not incorporate recent scientific insights.

A Conceptual Strategy

The conceptual problem analysis enables social psychologists to look for theories that could be fruitfully applied to the problem. Through association techniques the problem is translated into another set of more abstract and generic problems which may have been reported in the social psychological literature (see the Glossary). These problems can be used as key words in an electronic database search, like PsycINFO, PsychARTICLES, or Web of Science. Also, one could look at relevant social psychology textbooks for information about these topics. In the case of so-called emergency helping, through association with key terms such as 'altruism' and 'prosocial behaviour', we found bystander intervention theory and social dilemmas. In the STD example, one could look for associated words such as 'health', 'risk', 'vulnerability', 'optimism', and 'peer pressure'.

The difference between a topical and a conceptual strategy is sometimes minor. A social psychologist taking a topical perspective to explore how victims of accidents cope in the aftermath of the event will quickly discover that one of the more commonly used social psychological models to explain coping with accidents is **attribution theory** (Weiner, 1990), a theory that he might also come across with the conceptual strategy. Attribution research into coping with accidents shows that victims cope better with the consequences if they perceive themselves at least in part to blame for their misfortune. As another example of this overlap, in trying to explain the lack of enthusiasm for sustainable transport use, researchers will quickly find in the literature a reference to theories about social dilemmas (Van Vugt et al., 1995; 2000).

In the STD example, a conceptual strategy might result in a list of social psychological terms such as 'risk', 'risk perception', '**cognition**', 'optimism', 'health promoting behaviours', 'habit', 'negotiation and power', and '**self-efficacy**'. Once such a list has been prepared, one could then examine the social psychological literature for further information about these concepts. We will give just two examples of how a conceptual approach might inform the search for explanations of inconsistent condom use.

First, research on cognitive biases shows that people generally underestimate the chance that something bad will happen to them, like an illness, while overestimating the chance that something good will happen to them like winning the lottery. This is called 'unrealistic optimism' (Weinstein & Klein, 1996) and it may apply to the way teenagers think about contracting STD. Although this phenomenon might not have been studied in relation to STD, it has been studied for a range of other health-related behaviours and so it is plausible that the same mechanism might be at work in our example. Further reading on unrealistic optimism suggests that: (a) young people are more likely to hold such beliefs than old people, (b) optimism is generally higher with regard to bad things than good things, and (c) optimism is higher with behaviours that are controllable than uncontrollable (Rutter, Quine & Albery, 1998; Sparks, Shepherd, Wieringa & Zimmermans, 1995). These results suggest that this theory may be meaningfully applied to the safe sex example.

Second, the literature on negotiation and bargaining (Bazerman, Curhan, Moore & Valley, 2000; Thompson, 2006) suggests that individuals with less power in a relationship have more difficulties in negotiating a good deal. Power is related to how much people depend upon a relationship, both materially and psychologically. Having many opportunities to fulfil needs outside a relationship increases people's power position. Based on this research, social psychologists would expect that condom use might be affected by the power position that teenagers have in their relationship. People who feel less powerful might not want to discuss condom use with their partner although they might be aware of the benefits of it.

There are many other examples of how the conceptual approach might lead to explanations of inconsistent condom use. The risk perception literature suggests, for example, that people underestimate risks that are statistically small, and which involve a one-time activity, such as sexual intercourse (Linville, Fischer & Fischhoff, 1993). This implies that, although the chances of contracting STD are small without a condom, people tend to believe they are invulnerable. Alternatively, research suggests that habits are difficult to change, in part, because people do not attend to information criticizing the habit (Verplanken & Aarts, 1999). This suggests that once people have established a habit of not using condoms, changing this habit through intervention might be very difficult indeed.

These examples show that the essence of the conceptual approach is to use the problem definition to find concepts that are related to the problem. These concepts can then be used to find relevant theories that make predictions about the social psychological processes underlying a particular problem. The main advantage is that it can lead to a rich pattern of explanations, each of which can be elaborated further using appropriate theories and research. Furthermore, from the relevant theories, it is much easier to think of a set of interventions to tackle the problem. The main disadvantage is, of course, that it is easy to get overwhelmed by a multitude of theories. A social psychologist must therefore make an important decision about what he will focus on in the subsequent steps of the PATH model.

A General Theory Strategy

The general theory strategy analyses the problem through the lens of some very generic psychological theories. A model that, perhaps due to its simplicity, is often used in applied research is the theory of **reasoned action** (Ajzen, 1991; Ajzen & Fishbein, 2000). This attitude theory primarily focuses on behaviour that is under people's volitional control. The theory assumes that people's actions are shaped by their intentions. The intention to behave in a certain way is a product of people's attitudes and the social norms associated with the behaviour. Attitudes are a function of both the beliefs about the consequences of the action and also the subjective evaluation of these consequences. Social norms refer to the importance of the social environment and in particular what relevant people think of a person behaving in a certain way. The social norm is a product of the beliefs that relevant others have about the behaviour (normative beliefs) and people's motivation to comply with the beliefs of relevant others.

⊡ KT

Applied to the safe sex example, a social psychologist could try to establish whether condom use is under volitional control, and, if so, what are the relevant attitudes and social norms. For example, they might hypothesize that many teenagers have a belief that condoms reduce the pleasure of sex (belief) and that they highly value pleasurable sexual intercourse (evaluation). Furthermore, they might predict that many teenagers find it important what their peers think about condom use (motivation to comply) and that they believe their peers do not value condom use much (normative belief). This should then result in a negative intention towards condom use, which could explain the failure to use them. A social psychologist could try to back this up with pilot research to find out whether this is true or not. They could also look at a range of other consequences of condom use (for example, the risk of contracting an STD) to find out what teenagers think of these consequences and how they value them.

There are many other general theoretical models that could be fruitfully applied to generate explanations (see the Glossary). For example, in studying anti-social behaviour, social psychologists could rely on **rational choice theories** to examine the cost and reward structure of a particular anti-social behaviour such as creating graffiti (Becker & Mehlkop, 2006). They might find that youngsters believe that they are not going to get caught by the police because they create graffiti at night. Also, if they are caught they

⊡ KT

may think they will get away with a warning. Another general entry can be found in applying principles from evolutionary theory, which assumes that people are engaging in actions that maximize their survival and reproductive opportunities (Darwin, 1871). From this point of view, vandalism and hooliganism may be seen as so-called 'low status strategies', that is strategies for individuals who have lost in social competition and find themselves at the bottom of the societal hierarchy. For these individuals vandalism may be a form of aggression directed at more powerful others – authorities, the police – against whom they have no chance of winning.

In a similar vein, evolutionary psychology theory can be fruitfully applied to a host of different problems in society such as bad leadership, male violence, intergroup prejudice, sexual jealousy, organ donation, and environmental pollution (see for example, Buunk, Dijkstra & Massar, 2007; Schaller, Simpson & Kenrick, 2006; Van Vugt, 2006; Van Vugt, De Cremer & Janssen, 2007). Evolutionary psychology may be relevant for the analysis of so many problems because it uses a fundamentally different perspective than other theories. Evolutionary theory tries to uncover the *ultimate* reasons behind phenomena (that is, what their function is in human survival and reproduction), whereas other theories present explanations at a more *proximate* level of analysis. For instance, rational choice theory explains vandalism by referring to the belief that it is easy to avoid punishment, without explaining *why* someone endorses this belief or what they (unconsciously) gain from it. An evolutionary-minded social psychologist may 'dig' a little deeper and find out why the problem of vandalism is so persistent. This may then offer an important starting point for an intervention. For instance, attempts to influence anti-social activities may not be effective if youngsters feel they can impress their mates and potential sexual partners by engaging in such activities.

General theories of human social behaviour like attitude models, rational choice and evolutionary theories do not always lead to specific explanations for a problem. Their primary use is heuristic in the sense that they offer a new way of thinking about the causes of a problem. They need to be complemented with insights from other strategies and, where possible, with data from observations and interviews. Nevertheless, they offer some structure in analysing a particular problem and in understanding where the gaps in knowledge lie. For instance, when using evolutionary psychology to come up with possible causes for a problem, a social psychologist should ask himself what the function of a specific behaviour may be in the context of human survival and reproduction. Although he may conclude that hooliganism is a way to vent aggression, he may not yet know why, for instance, youngsters do not use other tactics like participating in martial arts. Through association, interviews and observations the social psychologist may fill in these knowledge gaps.

Sometimes it does not really matter which theoretical framework is selected as long as there is a framework to hang on to. This theory will then generate new clues about what to do next. For instance, despite their different perspectives, both social stress theories and evolutionary psychology theories may lead a social psychologist to look into the literature on aggression and/or self-esteem.

Epilogue

The previous examples show that there is a range of theoretical perspectives that can be thought of in analysing the causes of a particular problem. It may sometimes look like a random search process but this is not the case. On the basis of the problem definition a social psychologist will at least have a hunch in which directions he or she must look for relevant theories. However, at this stage the search for explanations needs to be open, without confining oneself too quickly to certain concepts or theories.

THE CONVERGENT PHASE: REDUCING THE NUMBER OF EXPLANATIONS

The aim of the divergent phase is to produce as many explanations as possible. In contrast, in the convergent phase the number of explanations is drastically reduced so that only the most plausible explanations remain. There are three different stages in the convergent phase. First, the number of explanations is reduced by getting rid of irrelevant and redundant explanations. Second, the theoretical validity of each of the remaining explanations is tested. Third, the remaining explanations are checked for their plausibility to account for the problem. This results in a smaller set of explanations that can be used in the next two phases of the PATH model – developing and testing a process model (Chapter 4) and setting up a help programme (Chapter 5). It is important to end up with a set of explanations that describe the social psychological processes leading to a problem in sufficient detail. One should avoid ending up with a set of 'dead end' explanations like 'teenagers who fail to use contraceptives are less intelligent'.

Getting Rid of Redundant and Irrelevant Explanations

Redundant Explanations

After the divergent phase, it will appear that there are various redundant or overlapping explanations for the problem. For example, through association and interviewing, a social psychologist may find that members of a production team feel their complaints are not taken seriously by the management, unlike complaints from other divisions. An inspection of the social psychological literature, using the topical and conceptual approaches, reveals a relation between procedural justice and employee satisfaction (Brennan & Kline, 2000; Martin & Brennett, 1996). These two explanations can then be combined into one, a concern about fair treatment among employees. Or alternatively, applying the theory of reasoned action to the problem of recruiting organ donors has identified that people might find it problematic to carry the donor registration form with them at all times (Brug, Van Vugt, Van den Borne, Brouwers & Van Hooff, 2000). This very problem might have also been brought up through examining the costs and benefits of donor registration via social exchange theory (see the Glossary).

Irrelevant Explanations

While in the divergent stage one may freely generate explanations, on further examination, some of these may appear to be irrelevant. In explaining why jurors in a particular trial appeared to be biased toward the defendant, a social psychologist may have assumed that pre-trial publicity might have played a role. If subsequent research shows that there were no media reports about the case prior to it then this explanation can be dismissed, even though the effects of pre-trial publicity are well documented (Kramer & Kerr, 1989)

Although reducing the number of explanations is important, one needs to be careful not to dismiss explanations that affect the outcome variable indirectly. Such explanations may provide important background information on the causes of the problem, and are important for building a process model. For example, in understanding an upsurge in male-to-male homicide in the UK, the social psychologist might come up with explanations having to do with frustration, poverty, **relative deprivation**, and gun and knife possession. A factor that might affect these more proximate explanations is that men are very status conscious, and willing to take fairly large risks in order to get what they want, even if that involves killing someone (Daly & Wilson, 2001). Because these types of account affects the problem – homicide – via their influence on other factors, like gun possession, they are particularly useful for developing a process model (see Chapter 4).

Getting Rid of Invalid Explanations

Theoretical explanations are only usefully applicable to a problem if the theory is valid under the conditions of the problem. For example, to apply social dilemma theory (Van Vugt, 1998) to a particular social problem, it must be shown that the characteristics of the problem are, in fact, a social dilemma. A social dilemma refers to a situation in which the rational pursuit of self-interest can lead to collective disaster (Komorita & Parks, 1994). According to social dilemma theory, a problem is only a social dilemma when two conditions are met, namely, with regard to the particular situation that, firstly selfishness has to be more attractive than cooperation, and secondly, that selfishness by all has to make everyone worse off in the long run (Dawes & Messick, 2000). Framed in this way, it seems inappropriate to use a social dilemma framework to explain why some drug addicts continue to commit street robberies even though they know that they will be caught and put in prison. The benefits of the selfish act (committing a robbery) do not outweigh the cost (that selfishness is more attractive than cooperation) and so a social dilemma explanation cannot easily be invoked.

It should be kept in mind that many social psychological theories are described in very generic terms, but really only apply to specific situations. A review of the scientific literature tells you under what conditions the theory has been tested and proven to work. **Cognitive dissonance theory** (Festinger, 1957; see the Glossary), for example, assumes that when people experience dissonance between their beliefs (for example, 'I want to be a reliable worker') and their behaviour (for example, 'I am often late for work') they will try to reduce this dissonance by changing their beliefs. The theory, however, states quite clearly that this will only happen if people think that they are personally responsible for their action (Cooper & Fazio, 1984). If they don't believe they are responsible, then they should not experience dissonance (for instance, you arrive late for work because of traffic congestion).

Another classic example is social comparison theory (Festinger, 1954; see the Glossary). This generic social psychological theory states that people, when comparing themselves to their peers in terms of their abilities, frequently make upward social comparisons, that is, they compare themselves to people slightly better than them. Research has overwhelmingly supported this prediction, but many results were obtained in one experimental setting only (Wheeler & Suls, 2005). In this setting, a number of participants took an ability test and then received feedback about their test score. False feedback ensures that they always occupy the middle position in their group. The scores of the other group members were not given. The participants then got a chance to look at the score of one other member of their group. Participants usually chose the group member with the next-best score, lending support to the upward comparison tendency, as predicted by social comparison theory.

Given the restrictions of the research paradigm, to what situations could this theory be meaningfully applied? Suppose a company asks a social psychologist about the implications of making public what managers in the company earn. The social psychologist turns to social comparison theory and predicts that employees will be primarily concerned about the earnings of staff members that are one level higher up the echelon and that they are relatively less concerned about the salaries of the board of directors. This may be what the theory predicts, but given that in experiments on this theory people have only been allowed to look at the salary of one other person (or group), this conclusion might be slightly premature. It is very well possible that, when given the opportunity, employees will also compare their salary with that of the directors. Translating the results of internally valid experiments into applicable knowledge about real-world problems is a recurrent concern of any applied social psychologist (see for example, Aronson et al., 2002; Brehm et al., 2005; Kenrick et al., 2005).

Finding the conditions under which a particular theory is applicable is an important task because it helps social psychologists decide on whether the theory can be fruitfully applied to a particular problem. In general, it is not enough to simply read the theory. Recent review articles can be helpful because they may give an updated summary of the state of a particular theory. However, usually one must look into how the experiments were conducted to find out about the theory's boundaries. Applying social psychological theories requires a basic knowledge about the research literature on a particular theory.

Getting Rid of Implausible Explanations

Finally, the plausibility of each of the explanations must be assessed. A particular explanation might be adequate in theory, but if it is not a likely cause of a problem then it can be dismissed. An example is neighbourhood recycling. Suppose a study reveals that only about 20 per cent of the residents in a neighbourhood regularly participate in the recycling of paper, glass and batteries. The applied psychologist could use the theory of reasoned action to find out why many are not taking part, for example, by focusing on anti-social norms in the neighbourhood (Cialdini & Trost, 1998). Interviews might reveal, however, that many residents simply do not know what they can and cannot recycle. This seemingly small obstacle could be a substantial barrier towards people participating so a social psychologist would do better to develop an information campaign (Guagnano, Stern & Dietz, 1995; Lyas, Shaw & Van Vugt, 2002). Note that such explanations might not need to be totally irrelevant to the problem (see 'Getting rid of redundant and irrelevant explanations' on pp. 76–77), but if they are unlikely to be substantial contributing factors, they can be dismissed easily.

The plausibility of an explanation can be established by carrying out a thought experiment. The aim of a thought experiment is to imagine what might happen if the particular condition that might cause the problem is either present or absent. Would there be a change in the outcome variable? If there is an outcome variable Z, a process variable Y, and a context variable X, then the reasoning is as follows: 'If this explanation is plausible, then in context X with process Y the result should be Z'. If the result is not Z, there are concerns about the plausibility of this explanation. Or an alternative reasoning is: 'If this explanation is plausible then, in the absence of Y, Z should not emerge in situation X'. Finding Z in that situation raises doubts about the plausibility of an explanation.

Consider this example. Friendly waiters receive larger tips from customers than unfriendly waiters (Lynn & Mynier, 1993; Van Baaren et al., 2003). A first explanation is that friendly waiters induce a good mood in diners, resulting in greater tipping. To determine the plausibility of this argument, it helps to think of analogous situations in which friendliness from one person increases a positive mood in another person, resulting in greater altruism towards the first person. For example, friendly teachers elicit positive emotions in students, which might make it more likely that they will try to maintain a good atmosphere in the classroom. In contrast, it is easy to think of situations in which an unfriendly face reduces the willingness to give. One only has to think of charity collectors who are a bit too pushy in asking for money. Could there be other ways to put people in a good mood and make them tip more, for example, by playing relaxing music in a restaurant or offering pleasant food? If so, there is another reason to support the mood hypothesis.

A second explanation is that customers tip friendly waiters more because they think the waiter likes them, perhaps more so than other customers. Many people are prepared to pay a little extra for 'royal' treatment. If this explanation is correct then customers should tip waiters less if they appear to be friendly to everyone. Now we can conduct a thought experiment in which we compare the two situations: a waiter who is friendly to all customers versus a waiter who is friendly to some customers only. In the latter case, we might be flattered but we might also doubt the professional integrity of the waiter and therefore tip less. Hence, there is a question mark about the validity of the 'royal' treatment explanation.

A third explanation is that customers perceive a smile or a friendly face as a gift, and they therefore feel obliged to reciprocate this favour. This **reciprocity** hypothesis is plausible if we can find other situations in which people feel they must return a favour by giving money when someone is friendly to them. There might be such situations, for example, when we donate to charity collectors who approach us with a friendly face. However, often we simply return a smile with a smile and there is no obligation to give money for a smile. It could be, of course, that friendliness is reciprocated with a tip only in restaurant settings. To test this hypothesis, a thought experiment can be carried out in which a customer returns a smile with a smile or in which the customer is the first to smile. In those cases, there should be less need to give a tip according to the obligation hypothesis. As this appears to be rather implausible, this explanation can be effectively ignored.

KT

Of course, thought experiments such as these do not produce any hard evidence. Therefore it is unwise to rely solely upon them. However, thought experiments do make it easier to select the most relevant causes for a problem. They may also serve as a basis for conducting further interviews or observations that reveal the most likely causes for the problem. In addition, it must be noted that most social psychological phenomena are based on a rather complex interaction between various different factors. Thus, it is important to concentrate on several plausible explanations in developing and testing a process model (Chapter 4) and setting up an intervention programme (Chapter 5).

Box 3.4   The Analysis Phase: Generating Theory-Based Explanations

In order to come up with scientifically valid explanations for a problem you have to take the following steps.

1. Specify the outcome variable in terms of a behaviour, attitude, or emotion (or a combination of them). Then pick an outcome variable which is relevant, sufficiently specific, concrete, and which can be described in continuous terms. Focus on one outcome variable at a time.
2. Try to generate explanations through association techniques. Don't be too critical at this stage. Try to come up with at least five different explanations for the problem.
3. Conduct real or hypothetical 'why' interviews to find the causes for the problem. By asking such questions as 'Why does this happen?', 'What do you think causes this?' and 'Who is responsible?', the processes underlying the problem might become clearer. When possible, conduct observations.
4. Try to come up with theory-based explanations for the problem. Use both a topical approach as well as a conceptual, and general theory, approach by looking at relevant social psychological theories.
5. Reduce the number of explanations through:

   - combining redundant explanations and eliminating irrelevant explanations;
   - inspecting the validity of theory-based explanations;
   - checking the plausibility of the explanations (through real or 'thought' experiments).

SUGGESTED FURTHER READING

Brug, J., Van Vugt, M., Van den Borne, B., Brouwers, A. & Van Hooff, H. (2000). Predictors of willingness to register as an organ donor among Dutch adolescents. *Psychology & Health, 15(3)*, 357–368.

Gardner, G. T. & Stern, P. C. (1996). *Environmental Problems and Human Behaviour*. Boston: Allyn & Bacon.

Manstead, A. J. & Hewstone, M. (1996). *The Blackwell Encyclopedia of Social Psychology*. London: Blackwell.

Schaller, M., Simpson, J. & Kenrick, D. (2006). *Evolution and Social Psychology*. New York: Psychology Press.

ASSIGNMENT 3

A team of marital therapists asks you, as a social psychologist, for advice. In general, the team is confronted with couples with numerous marital problems, such as a lack of emotional intimacy, jealousy and physical or verbal aggression. Most of these problems can be effectively dealt with in couple therapy. However, the team has observed that there is also a large group of couples who share a similar communication problem that often results in relationship dissatisfaction and that may ultimately lead to divorce. One of the marital therapists reports an example of a recent couple therapy session that illustrates this problem (example taken from Kline, Pleasant, Whitton & Markman, 2006).

> The wife, Sally (42), describes what happened over the weekend when she tried to talk to her husband, Scott (45), about landscaping their yard. She said that she asked Scott (while he was reading the newspaper) how much money he thought they could spend and whether he was leaning toward rose bushes or rhododendrons at the front. She apparently then replied in a somewhat agitated voice: 'Well, I need your input because we have to talk about how much we can spend'. Scott continued reading his newspaper. He reported during the session that he could tell his wife had become angry and that he did not want to make things worse by talking. He reported that he felt that anything he said would have made her more mad, so he chose to be silent and let her have time to calm herself down. What Sally did, though, was become even angrier, saying: 'Why don't you ever listen to me'?! Scott reported that he then told her he was going for a walk alone because their conversation was going nowhere. The issue then switched from being one about money to communication and caring. Sally was clearly pursuing Scott and demanding that they discuss an issue which was important to her and Scott was withdrawing, later explaining in the session that he did so because he did not know how to react to Sally in a way that would not make her angrier. Sally told the therapist that Scott's silence about things was exactly what made her most angry in their relationship.

This type of communication is called the demand-withdraw pattern and refers to a pattern of communication in which one spouse nags or complains while the other spouse avoids or withdraws from the conflict discussion. Because so many couples that seek help seem to suffer from this problem, the therapists wondered whether it is possible to help these couples by means of a different intervention than couple therapy. They now ask the social psychologist involved to develop an alternative means of helping these couples.

(a) Formulate a problem definition according to Chapter 2's criteria (see Box 2.4, pp. 52–53).
(b) Specify the outcome variable in terms of behaviour, attitude and/or emotions. The outcome variable must be relevant to the problem as well as specific, concrete and continuous.
(c) Try to generate as many explanations as possible (at least five!) for the problem by means of problem and concept association and perspective taking. Don't be too critical and selective in the first instance.
(d) Conduct two imaginary 'why' interviews to find out what process may underlie the problem: one with a marital therapist and one with Sally. Vary your questions (for example, 'What makes you think that?', 'What is it about that that … ?', 'Why do you think that?').

(e) Generate as many theoretical explanations as you can on the basis of:

- attribution theory;
- social exchange theory;
- learning theory;
- stress theory.

(f) Reduce the number of explanations by:

- getting rid of irrelevant and redundant explanations;
- testing the theoretical validity of each of the remaining explanations;
- checking the remaining explanations for their plausibility in accounting for the problem by using thought experiments.

CHAPTER 4

THE TEST PHASE: DEVELOPING AND TESTING THE PROCESS MODEL

Contents

The Test Phase: Developing and Testing the Process Model

INTRODUCTION

Once a set of explanations has been identified and selected by a social psychologist, he or she then develops a process model. This model serves as a template for developing interventions. In this chapter, we discuss the third step of the PATH model, the Test phase. In this stage we make suggestions on how to develop the process model and how to test the empirical validity of the model.

FORMULATING A PROCESS MODEL

The explanations selected in Chapter 3 form the core of the process model. A raw version of a process model may have been developed in the previous stage already, for example, in the 'why' interview (Chapter 2). A process model is a *pictorial representation of the explanatory variables, and their relationships with each other and with the focal problem* (see Figure 4.1, p. 86). Each variable is represented as a box. The boxes (the variables) in the model are connected via arrows. The valence of an arrow indicates whether there is a positive (+) or negative (−) relationship between two variables. Formulating a process model helps social psychologists to develop a structured account of the problem and its underlying causes. It should also give clues as to where interventions must be targeted in the model.

There are a number of general guidelines for developing a process model. We illustrate these with two cases:

1. improving the cooperation among divisions in a pharmaceutical company;
2. reducing the risk of infection with a sexually transmitted disease (STD).

In both examples, the process model is formulated using relevant social psychological theories that are generated via the topical, conceptual, and general theory strategies that we discussed in the previous chapter.

Case Study: Improving Cooperation in a Pharmaceutical Company

The Problem Definition

A large pharmaceutical firm in the UK spends around £5 million (8 million euros) a year on research and development. The board of directors (*for whom is it a problem?*) believes the returns are insufficient. The director of Research and Development (R& D) has been told to increase the number of useful ideas and products, otherwise the division will face budget cuts and job losses (*why is it a problem?*). The director (*for whom is it a problem?*) believes the problem may be due to a lack of teamwork among the scientists in the division's laboratories. She feels that they prefer to work on their own hobbies rather than collaborate to create commercially successful products for the company (*what is the problem?*). In addition, she feels that there is poor communication between the scientists and the people in marketing who must judge the saleability of their products (*what is the problem?*). The director wonders how she could facilitate cooperation among the scientists such that the productivity of the division is raised, and they can avoid downsizing. She knows from other pharmaceutical companies that research divisions that have a more cooperative work structure tend to be more successful. She asks a team of applied psychologists to examine the problem and offer suggestions to improve team cooperation.

The Analysis

Based on interviews with the director and the scientists at the firm, the applied psychologists realize that the success of the R&D division is dependent upon scientists working closely together on developing a narrow range of new products and ideas. They are also aware that this is not necessarily in each scientist's interest. Each of them would presumably rather work on developing their own products rather than helping to develop someone else's products, even though the latter might be better from the company's point of view. From this analysis, the psychologists conclude that they have to find ways to resolve this conflict of interests in order to facilitate cooperation. They turn to the social psychological literature for answers and find a paradigm that might be useful: the *social dilemma* paradigm. A social dilemma is a situation in which individuals with competing interests damage the collective interest (see Chapter 3). If many individuals pursue their narrow, selfish interests, the collective suffers and in the end everyone will be worse off. The social dilemma literature identifies many different factors that facilitate group cooperation (Kerr & Tindale, 2004; Komorita & Parks, 1994; Van Vugt, 1998).

The psychologists believe that the problem in R&D is essentially a social dilemma and examine the literature for clues. They find that cooperation in social dilemmas is promoted through offering selective (financial) incentives for cooperation (Van Vugt, 1998). They also find that better communication facilitates teamwork and people work better together if they identify more strongly with their team (Dawes, Van de

Figure 4.1   A preliminary process model: What determines cooperation in this company?

Kragt & Orbell, 1988). Together, these factors promote the commitment that people feel toward their group, which, in turn, increases team cooperation and productivity (Kerr, 1989; Dovidio et al., 2006).

Developing a Process Model

How to develop a process model on the basis of these explanations? First, we must be clear about the outcome variable. What is it that we wish to influence or improve? Ideally, this has already been done in the previous steps of the PATH model, but perhaps there is a concern that the outcome variable is still not concrete enough. For example, the generic term 'cooperation' could be turned into something more specific like 'willingness to help your colleagues'.

Next, we must draw up a diagram of the preliminary process model (see Figure 4.1). We can put the outcome variable in a box to the right of the figure. Subsequently, we will select one of the possible explanations for the problem. The social dilemma literature suggests that the primary cause of competition among the scientists lies in the nature of the task – competition for new products and ideas – and that this inhibits cooperation (Van Lange & De Dreu, 2001). Thus, a first sketch of the process model might look something like this figure.

This looks like a plausible first model, but there are several problems with it. First, the explanatory factor ('nature of the task') is not described as a continuous and quantitative variable (see Chapter 3). It is unclear how this variable could vary from less to more, and therefore how exactly it is related to the outcome variable ('cooperation'). Is there a positive or negative relationship between 'nature of task' and 'cooperation'? One could draw a distinction between different kinds of tasks, for example, cooperative versus competitive tasks (Steiner, 1972), but they are still not continuous.

A second problem is that some of the variables are still too general. It is unclear how the 'nature of the task' might affect cooperation among scientists in R&D. Furthermore, as we have said earlier, the term 'cooperation' could be made more specific. A more concrete description would be 'willingness to help colleagues' because this will ultimately be the aim of an intervention programme.

An improved model would use more concrete terms to describe the variables. For example, the nature of the task would be translated into several specific and continuous task elements. One of them relates to the fact that the scientists compete with each other to develop the best and most useful products. This variable could be described as 'competition between scientists'. Furthermore, as they all have their own labs there is little coordination between the scientists, hence 'degree of coordination of task activities'

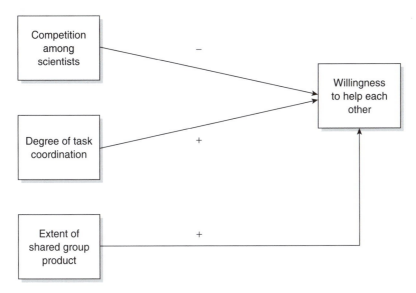

Figure 4.2   An improved process model: What determines cooperation in this company?

may also be included in the process model. Finally, once a product idea is endorsed by the company, it is developed further by one of the labs. Thus, there is little evidence of a shared team product ('the degree of shared group product'). These are all related to the end variable, which we could describe more concretely as 'willingness to help colleagues'. The improved process model is depicted in Figure 4.2.

The arrows depict the direction of the relationships and the valence of the relationships in the model could be described as well. Because there is likely to be a negative relationship between 'competition' and 'willingness to help' each other, we put a minus (–) sign there. Conversely, the 'extent of shared group product' correlates positively with 'willingness to help', hence the positive (+) sign. Finally, the 'degree of task coordination' should correlate positively with 'willingness to help' (+). The valence of these relationships can normally be estimated through common sense, but sometimes consulting the literature can be helpful too.

This second model is a substantial improvement yet it is still lacking in details about the process leading to the manifestation of the problem. We have now identified three task-related characteristics that might cause the problem, but we do not know whether they have a direct or indirect influence on the problem. In other words, does A cause B directly or, does A influence B via its effect upon C? For example, poor coordination of task activities presumably leads to poor communication between scientists, and this in turn affects the absence of a helping culture in R&D. The social dilemma research suggests that communication promotes cooperation (Van Vugt, 1998), so this is clearly an important intermediate factor. Similarly, the absence of a shared group product may lead the scientists to not feel very responsible for the activities of the research team as a whole. Thus, a 'shared group product' might influence willingness to help via an

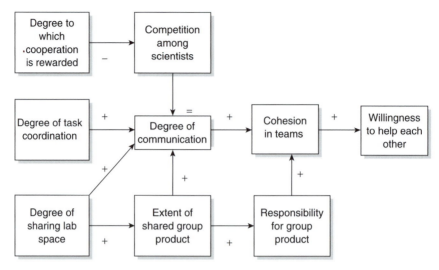

Figure 4.3   Improved process model 2: What factors determine cooperation within this company?

increased 'responsibility for the group product' that scientists feel. In turn, all these factors may undermine team cohesion within the division, which could be the proximate cause of an unwillingness to help each other.

In addition, the variables introduced in Figure 4.2 might in turn be caused by other factors. For example, salaries tend to depend upon each scientist's personal achievements (how many product ideas they have developed in their labs), which probably creates a climate of excessive competition between individuals. In turn, this might affect the cohesion of the team and their willingness to help each other. Furthermore, the fact that each scientist has their own laboratory may make it difficult for them to coordinate their activities and appreciate that there is ultimately a shared group product. This leads to a much improved model, depicted in Figure 4.3.

If we work our way backwards then this model suggests that the willingness to help each other in the R&D division is undermined by poor team cohesion. This, in turn, is affected by the absence of sufficient communication between scientists and the absence of feelings of personal responsibility for the group product. These factors in return are caused, ultimately, by an excessive competition between the scientists (perhaps due to the salary system) and by the absence of task coordination and of a shared group product (perhaps due to each scientist only working in their own lab).

This is one possible way to construct a process model, but it is certainly not the only way. In general, it takes a lot of time and adjustment to come up with a process model that describes the relationships between the variables as precisely and completely as possible. It is worth it because a good process model should give a clear recommendation regarding the nature of interventions necessary to tackle the problem. For example, as a result of their process analysis, the psychologists might recommend to the director that laboratories should be shared, where possible, so that scientists communicate more with each other, thereby learning to work together on each other's ideas.

Box 4.1   Interview with Professor Michael West of the Aston Business School (UK)

'When I finished my PhD in psychology, I worked underground as a labourer for a year in a coal mine, in order to earn money to pay off student debts. Once I got over my fear of working in such a dangerous environment, I became fascinated by the teamworking and camaraderie that are necessary for safety and effectiveness in such a hostile environment. That experience shaped much of my subsequent interest in applied social and organizational psychology. Research too is about teamworking and vigorous collaboration across boundaries.

'Since my work in the coal mine, I have worked at colleges all over the world: among others, at the University of Kent (UK), the Bermuda College (Bermuda), the University of Queensland (Australia) and the Technical University of Eindhoven (The Netherlands). Since joining Aston Business School in 1999, I have bridged many more boundaries (disciplinary and international) and feel privileged to work in the domains and with the wide variety of colleagues that academic life offers.

'In general, my work in social/organizational psychology has been applied with a particular focus on influencing organizational and public policy. I am currently running an annual survey for the English National Health Service on staff attitudes and experiences and linking the findings to outcomes such as patient mortality, patient satisfaction, errors and staff behaviours. It is very rewarding to see applied social and organizational psychological research being translated into government policies and thereby positively affecting patient care.

'For the future I foresee an important role for social psychology in the field of ageing. The ageing of the population is a major change in society and social psychologists must urgently engage with this currently neglected topic. In addition, globalization, international travel and migration make diversity a fundamentally important topic. And who better than social psychologists to explore and explain how we can make a strength and virtue of these changes? We must discover how we can successfully overcome the inherent pathology of inter-group prejudice which threatens our survival as a species. This requires understanding positive social processes associated with successful diversity and promulgating those far and wide.'

Interested in Professor West's work? Then read, for instance,:

West, M.A., Borrill, C.S. & Dawson, J.F. (2003). Leadership clarity and team innovation in health care. *Leadership Quarterly, 14(4–5)*, 393–410.

West, M.A. (2004) *The secrets of successful team management: How to lead a team to innovation, creativity and success*. London: Duncan Baird Publishers.

Figure 4.4   A preliminary process model: What determines condom use?

Case Study: Reducing the Risk of STD Infection

The Problem Definition

According to an estimate by UNAIDS in 2005 more than 26 million people world-wide are suffering from HIV/AIDS (see also Chapter 1). In Britain alone around 80,000 people are believed to be infected with the HIV virus. There is currently no cure or remedy available for HIV/AIDS. The only feasible strategy is to engage in behaviours that reduce one's risk of contracting HIV/AIDS. The main preventative behaviour is condom use. Condom use also protects against the transmission of other, less deadly, types of sexually transmitted diseases (STDs) such as chlamydia and gonorrhoea.

One particular health authority in a coastal area of Britain (*for whom is it a problem?*) has documented a rise in STDs (*what is the problem?*) among the young adult population. This is attributed to an increase in late night entertainment facilities in the city that attract a lot of youngsters to the area, particularly during the summer months (*causes of the problem*). It has been decided that there will be a campaign to promote safe sex practices among youngsters in the area, and the authorities decide to focus on condom use in particular. A team of health professionals and social psychologists is hired to set up a campaign to foster condom use and they begin by reviewing the relevant behavioural and psychological literature (see, for example, Adih & Alexander, 1999; Buunk et al., 1998; Helweg-Larsen & Collins, 1994; Schaalma, Kok & Peters, 1993; Sheeran, Abraham & Orbell, 1999; Sheeran & Taylor, 1999). From this literature, several potential causes appear for the failure to use condoms:

- A lack of awareness about STDs, and the relation between STDs and unprotected sex.
- People don't believe they are at risk of contracting an STD, possibly because they use other contraceptives, such as the pill.
- People think that sex without condoms somehow 'feels better'.
- People believe their partner is not bothered about using a condom.
- People do not bring up condom use, possibly because they are too embarrassed or they think their partner will reject them.
- People are too drunk to consider using a condom.
- People do not bring condoms when they go out.

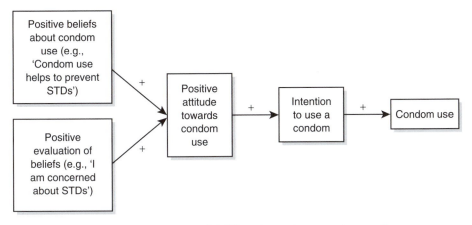

Figure 4.5   An improved process model: What determines condom use?

- People lack practice in putting on a condom.
- There is no positive inclination to use a condom.

In working towards an intervention programme to foster condom use, the psychologists decide to concentrate on two well-known attitude-behaviour models: the theory of reasoned action (TRA; Fishbein & Ajzen, 1975) and the **theory of planned behaviour** (TPB; Ajzen, 1987). They specify condom use as the outcome variable in their process model. Next they select a potential cause. The main determinant of condom use, according to these theories, is a positive intention to use a condom. Hence, the preliminary causal model that they draw up (see Figure 4.4) contains two factors.

KT

Of course, the main problem with this model is that it does not specify the underlying causes for not engaging in safe sex practices such as condom use. According to TRA and TPB, individuals' intentions are determined by their attitudes. The psychologists therefore first concentrate on the attitudes of youngsters towards condom use. According to TRA and TPB, the attitude is formed first by beliefs regarding the costs and benefits of not using a condom. For example, a potential cost would be susceptibility to contracting an STD, whereas a potential benefit would be that the sex is more pleasant. The second component of the attitude is the evaluation of these beliefs, for example, how much do people care about avoiding an STD or having a perfect sexual experience? This results in a more detailed process model such as the one sketched in Figure 4.5.

This looks like a better model, but there are still several problems with it. First, it ignores the fact that to engage in sexual intercourse requires the cooperation of another person (Kashima, Gallois & McCamish, 1993). Hence, it is probably also important what the sexual partner thinks about condom use. Furthermore, the decision to use a condom is probably also influenced by the wider social environment, for example, what someone's friends think about condom use, and perhaps what someone's parents might

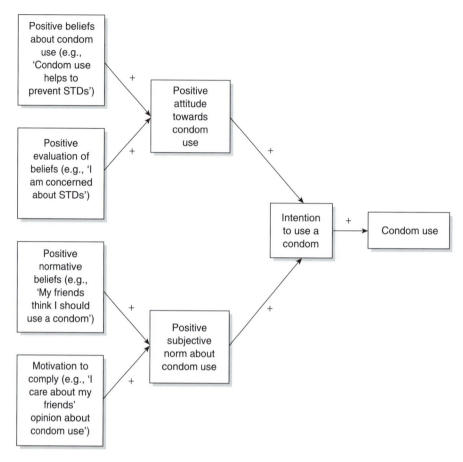

Figure 4.6   Improved process model 2: What determines condom use?

think. Thus, a more elaborate model would take these subjective (social) norms into account. In TRA and TPB the social norms consist of two components:

1. the attitude of relevant others (like parents or friends) toward condom use (so-called normative beliefs);
2. a motivation to comply with the attitudes of relevant others.

Thus, a more detailed model is depicted in Figure 4.6.

In many ways, this model looks like it offers many promising directions for setting up an intervention programme. However, it still ignores the fact that although young-sters may have positive attitudes towards condom use and the social norms might be conducive, there might still be important obstacles for the desired behaviour (Schaalma, Kok & Peters, 1993; Sheeran, Abraham & Orbell, 1999). An important obstacle may be that a person feels too incapable to put on a condom, for example, because of limited experience or perhaps because of drunkenness. TPB refers to these obstacles in terms of control beliefs (also called perceived behavioural control or 'self-efficacy'), namely

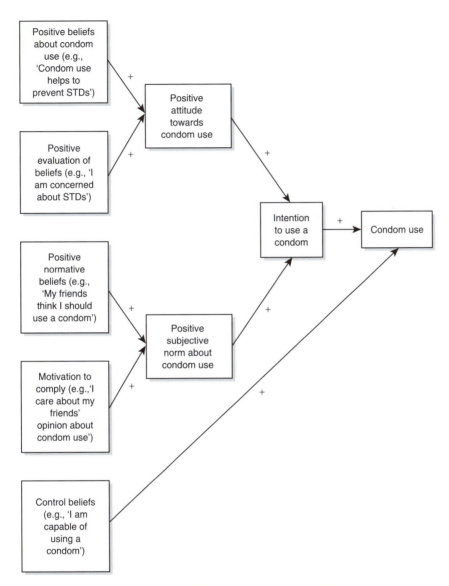

Figure 4.7   Improved process model 3: What determines condom use?

the belief that you can do something if you want to. Thus, we should add a box to the model which specifies the sense of control that teenagers feel over their condom use. This results in a model like Figure 4.7.

We have now analysed several different factors which presumably underlie condom use. Using TRA and TPB models, we have developed a process model in which the relevant behaviour (condom use) is shaped by control beliefs and intentions, with the latter being further influenced by attitudes and social norms. Each of these factors contains both belief and evaluation components. We could go further by going backward

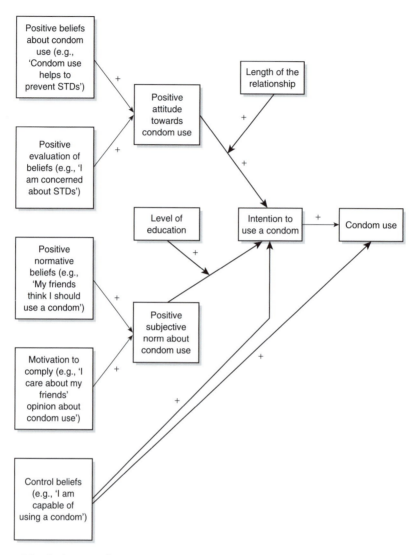

Figure 4.8   An improved process model 4: What determines condom use?

in the model and hypothesizing about factors influencing these attitudes and social norms. For example, it is likely that partners in long-term relationships will be less affected by their attitudes about unprotected sex, because for them the risk of contracting an STD is smaller. Furthermore, education level could increase the importance of social norms promoting condom use (Sheeran, Abraham & Orbell, 1999). So, we could add *length of the relationship* and *educational level* as distant variables in the model, interacting with more proximate psychological factors like attitudes and social norms. This is depicted by an arrow running from the reinforcing variable (for example, education level) to the arrow between two existing variables (see Figure 4.8). In addition, it could be argued that control beliefs exercise both an indirect effect on condom use, via shaping the intention, as well as a direct effect. For example, a positive intention towards using a condom might fail to materialize in the desired behaviour, because a person might simply have forgotten to bring a condom (Gage, 1998).

Thus, this example serves as a nice illustration of the development of a process model, because it contains four different effects:

- *Direct effects*: variations in one variable directly affect variations in another variable, for example, intentions affect condom use directly.
- *Indirect effects*: one variable affects another variable via a third variable. For example, the belief that condom use may prevent STD affects the behaviour by adding to the intention to use a condom.
- *Reinforcing effects*: one variable strengthens the impact of another variable on the behaviour. For example, education level might interact with subjective norms to produce a stronger effect on the intention to use condoms.
- *Undermining effects*: one variable mitigates the relationship between two other variables. For example, being in a long-term relationship might weaken the influence of positive attitudes on the intention to use a condom.

Box 4.2   A Case Study: Losing Weight

Being overweight is a problem of great concern. Currently, about 70 per cent of adults in the USA and 45 per cent of the adults in European countries, such as the Netherlands, are overweight (see digital infobase World Health Organization, www.who.int). Individuals who are overweight are at risk of developing serious medical conditions, such as hypertension and diabetes. In addition, obesity creates a major economic burden through loss of productivity and income and consumes about 10 per cent of overall health care budgets.

For many overweight individuals, efforts to lose weight meet with very limited success. Nonetheless, it can be done. Social psychologists Debora Schifter and Icek Ajzen from the University of Massachusetts wanted to uncover the differences between overweight individuals who succeed in losing weight and overweight individuals who do not*. They based their study on the theory of planned behaviour (TRB) and asked female participants who considered themselves to be overweight to fill in two questionnaires, one initially (Time 1) and another six weeks later (Time 2). Participants answered questions about their weight and rated items about attitudes towards losing weight (for example, 'For me to reduce weight during the next six weeks is desirable/undesirable'), a subjective norm (for example, 'To what extent do most people who are important to you think you should reduce weight over the next six weeks?'), intentions (for example, 'I intend to reduce weight over the next six weeks'), and control beliefs (for example, 'How likely is it that if you try you will manage to reduce weight over the next six weeks?').

(Continued)

After six weeks, the participants filled in another questionnaire that asked about their experiences during the preceding six weeks and their weight. The social psychologists found that no less than 58 per cent of the participants managed to lose weight during the six weeks of the study. Surprisingly, they also found that weight loss had little to do with the strength of women's intentions to lose weight (or, in other words, their motivation). A much better predictor of weight loss was the degree to which women believed they had control over their body weight. According to the social psychologists, individuals with perceived high control are more likely to try losing weight than are individuals with perceived low control, even if their perceptions are unrealistic. Those women who strongly intended to lose weight and also believed that they were capable of doing so were most likely to succeed.

Their study strongly suggests that intervention programmes for overweight individuals should not primarily focus on individuals' motivation to lose weight (for example, by pointing out the disadvantages of being overweight and the advantages of being slim) but instead, should try to strengthen individuals' beliefs that they can control their body weight.

Schifter, D.E. & Ajzen, I. (1985). Intention, perceived control, and weight loss: An application of the theory of planned behaviour. *Journal of Personality and Social Psychology, 49,* 843–851.

HEURISTICS FOR DEVELOPING A PROCESS MODEL

The above examples should help you to develop a process model, regardless of the particular behaviour being studied or explanation offered. These are examples of a way of thinking that is important for applying social psychology, which involves a considerable amount of logic and interpretation. Although there is not one particular blueprint for developing a process model, there are various heuristics that could be helpful in organizing a process model. The following 11 rules of thumb may help develop a process model:

1. Make a list of the possible explanations and variables involved.
2. Ensure that all these variables are social psychological, specific (rather than general), concrete (rather than abstract) and continuous rather than binary.
3. Ensure that these variables affect behaviours, attitudes, or motivations.
4. Draw up the outcome variable on the right-hand side of the process model.
5. Move from the right to the left-hand side of the model by asking yourself which variable influences the outcome variable.
6. Draw arrows between these variables to depict the direction of the relationship (+ = positive, − = negative, ? = don't know yet).

7. Make sure that the relationship between the variables is not too remote. Otherwise, consider putting in a mediating variable (for instance, in the condom use example, the attitude is likely to affect the behaviour via the intention).
8. When coming up with new variables think about whether they have direct effects, indirect effects, reinforcing or undermining effects on the other variables in the model.
9. When there are several variables influencing the outcome variable, work each of them out in detail and then consider whether they are related to each other. Draw an arrow between them if you think they are.
10. In practice, a process model should contain no more than about 10 variables (excluding the outcome variable) to make it workable. One should make sure the model is parsimonious, while at the same time providing sufficient detail about each of the explanations.
11. To develop a practical model there should not be too many steps between the outcome variable and the most distal variables. Aim for about four different steps to make it manageable.

TESTING THE PROCESS MODEL

In choosing a particular theory or set of theories, the applied social psychologist will often have already looked at the empirical literature for evidence. Particularly in the issue-related approach, it is often clear from research what the strength and direction of the relationships are between the variables in the model. Hence, there may already be a solid empirical basis for the model. Meta-analytic tests and review articles are most useful because they summarize the results of various studies on a particular topic. In the condom use example, the health psychologist finds an article that contains a very helpful and recent meta-analytic review of the psychological and behavioural correlates of condom use, entitled: 'Theories of reasoned action and planned behaviour as models of condom use: A **meta-analysis**.' The article is published in the scientific journal *Psychological* KT *Bulletin* and is written by psychologist Dolores Albarracín and her colleagues. This review suggests the correlations between the different variables shown in the model (see Figure 4.9).

It can be seen from this model that the intention to use a condom has a moderately strong positive influence on condom use (r = .45). Attitudes, subjective norms and control beliefs all have a moderately strong positive influence on the intention to use a condom (r = .58, r = .39, and r = .45 respectively). In a similar vein, attitudes are positively influenced by beliefs about condom use (r = .56) and subjective norms by normative beliefs (r = .46). Control beliefs also show a direct positive influence on condom use (r = .25). However, the article also shows that, after controlling for intentions, the direct influence of control beliefs on condom use becomes very small. That is, the influence of control beliefs on condom use can be explained almost entirely through their effect on intentions.

The psychologist may therefore decide to remove the arrow between control beliefs and condom use from the model. He may also search the literature for articles that do report evidence of a significant direct effect of control beliefs on condom use. If the psychologist finds such an article he should take a close look at the background variables of the study, such as the age and educational level of the participants. If these

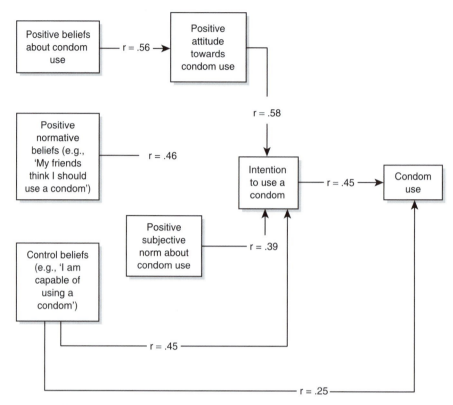

Figure 4.9   Empirical support for the process model

background variables are comparable with the characteristics of the situation and population the social psychologist aims to influence, he might decide to keep the arrow in the model, despite the negative conclusion of the review article. In a similar vein the social psychologist should try to find empirical support in the literature for all of the relationships in his process model.

Thus, it is important to examine the relationships between the model variables by consulting the empirical literature. This means that for every relationship in the model one must specify the strength and direction of the relationship. Obviously, the variables with the strongest influence are the most useful ones for an intervention, because a change in that variable is likely to lead to a significant change in the variables it influences.

How does one find relevant research? In seeking to find literature one could use one of the three approaches that we outlined in Chapter 3 to finding explanations: the topical, the conceptual, and the general theoretical approach. It is generally advisable to search for research that is directly relevant to the problem definition, thus the issue-related approach. The reason is that the relevance of the findings diminishes the greater the difference between the research and the problem the social psychologist is interested in. Although there are various literature search programmes available (like PsycINFO or Google scholar), it may not be easy to find all the available evidence. First, not all research is published and this is more likely for null effects, that is, research that supports the null hypothesis of no difference. It is therefore often useful to send a message to an email list of researchers in a particular field (like the SPSP or EAESP mailing lists for social psychologists).

Second, not all the published research is of the same relevance and quality so it is important to carefully read each article and judge their quality and relevance. Third, research articles may contradict each other in their results or conclusions. One's best bet is often a meta-analytic review of a research domain, which summarizes the available evidence and estimates the strengths of a particular effect across a broad domain of studies (as in the condom use example). Such meta-analytic reviews appear in journals like *Psychological Bulletin*, *Personality and Social Psychology Review*, *Health Psychology*, and *Health Education Quarterly*, and it is worth looking out for them.

Even if there is no research available on the topic of interest then it may still be useful to examine the literature. For example, a social psychologist may be interested in organizational citizenship behaviour, but because there is not yet a lot of research available on it, he may look instead at the broader helping literature for clues (Penner, Dovidio, Pilavin & Schroeder, 2005). But even if a conceptual approach does not work then a general theory approach might be helpful. For example, research on the Theory of Reasoned Action (TRA) or the Theory of Planned Behaviour (TPB) might be helpful even when the behaviours which are of interest are entirely different. For example, the knowledge that subjective norms are an important influence on smoking decisions, might help a social psychologist in thinking about what factors might influence recycling. Similarly, a general evolutionary psychological theory like reciprocal altruism might give an applied psychologist the suggestion that stress and burn-out in the workplace may be caused by feelings of inequity and unfairness (Buunk & Schaufeli, 1999).

DOING YOUR OWN RESEARCH

Unfortunately, not all the relationships in the model will have been documented in the research literature. For example, there simply may not be any existing research on the relationship between alcohol intake and condom use. Thus, it is important that, if necessary, social psychologists are able to do their own research to find answers. This book is not the place to discuss in any great detail the research methods needed for doing applied social psychological research. Each person studying for a degree in social psychology will have a solid training in research methods in psychology. And there are many good texts available on conducting social psychological research (see, for example, Breakwell, 2004; Reis & Judd, 2000).

The importance of doing research in answering an applied social psychological problem cannot be overstressed. Often, there is empirical literature on a particular topic but the research may not have been adequately done. Or else the research has tested a particular relationship in a slightly different domain than the one the social psychologist is interested in. For example, a psychologist interested in the determinants of using contraceptives cannot simply rely on the research on condom use. Nevertheless there may be important clues to be found in this literature. In addition, many field studies contain cross-sectional data (all gathered at the same time) and the resultant correlation between two variables may not indicate a causal relationship whereby one variable causes another. One must therefore be cautious in simply applying the results of other studies to the problem under investigation.

Furthermore, many studies in social psychology are laboratory-based, primarily with students as research participants. These studies are high in internal validity (that is, the results are reliable), but they are sometimes lacking in external validity (that is, the results may not be applicable to other situations and/or populations). Hence, one should consider the possibility that there are limitations in generalizing the results to apply to the real world. For example, some people might take task risks in the laboratory, gambling with small sums of money, but does it mean that they also take risks in real-world tasks like drug use, not wearing seatbelts or having unprotected sex? Even if results have been obtained in field research there is often the question of whether data can be generalized from one population to another. This is particularly important in cross-cultural research. Research suggests that American people differ from Asian people in the way they respond to social psychology experiments. American students, for example, see themselves as more independent whereas Japanese students see themselves as more interdependent (Kitayama, Markus, Matsumoto & Norasakkunkit, 1997). This difference might be relevant in finding strategies to promote, for instance, cooperation in the workplace or at school.

In conducting research to establish the validity of a process model, it can be useful to conduct a quick survey. In survey research, the main variables are operationalized and measured and then through statistical procedures the researcher determines the relationship between the variables. Whenever possible, researchers use existing scales of variables that have been tested in previous research and reported in the psychological literature. An example of a commonly used scale is Rosenberg's self-esteem scale (containing 10 items) which is depicted in Box 4.3. This can be used in a school, sports, or work environment.

Box 4.3   Rosenberg's Self-Esteem Scale (Rosenberg, 1965)

Below is a list of statements dealing with your general feelings about yourself. If you strongly agree, circle SA. If you agree with the statement, circle A. If you disagree, circle D. If you strongly disagree, circle SD.

1. On the whole, I am satisfied with myself.	SA	A	D	SD
2.* At times, I think I am no good at all.	SA	A	D	SD
3. I feel that I have a number of good qualities.	SA	A	D	SD
4. I am able to do things as well as most other people.	SA	A	D	SD
5.* I feel I do not have much to be proud of.	SA	A	D	SD
6.* I certainly feel useless at times.	SA	A	D	SD
7. I feel that I'm a person of worth, at least on an equal plane with others.	SA	A	D	SD

8.* I wish I could have more respect for myself.   SA   A   D   SD
9.* All in all, I am inclined to feel that I am a failure.   SA   A   D   SD
10. I take a positive attitude toward myself.   SA   A   D   SD

Scoring: SA = 3, A = 2, D = 1, SD = 0. Items with an asterisk are reverse scored, that is, SA = 0, A = 1, D = 2, SD = 3. Sum the scores for the 10 items. The higher the score, the higher the self-esteem.

Another example of a commonly used scale is the PANAS (Watson, Clark & Tellegen, 1988), which contains 20 items and measures one's emotional state. Normally, researchers first determine the reliability of a scale using a Cronbach's alpha index that may run from 0 to 1. In social research a Cronbach's alpha of .70 or higher is considered acceptable. It means that the items on the scale all measure the same underlying construct, and that therefore the scale is reliable. The social psychologist may then use a median split to categorize the sample into those with a low level and those with a high level of the trait under investigation in order to compare the two groups on a dependent variable. For example, when a social psychologist wants to know whether individuals with low self-esteem experience different emotions than individuals with high self-esteem, she could ask individuals to fill in a questionnaire that assesses their self-esteem (Box 4.3) and their emotions on a certain day (Box 4.4). After having established that the Cronbach alphas for the two scales are satisfactory, she could then divide the group of participants in half: individuals with low self-esteem and individuals with high self-esteem. With a t-test or analysis of variance she could calculate to what extent individuals with low self-esteem experience different emotions than individuals with high self-esteem.

Box 4.4   The Positive and Negative Affect Schedule (PANAS; Watson, Clark & Tellegen, 1988)

This scale consists of 20 words that describe different feelings and emotions. Read each item and then mark the appropriate number in the space next to that word. Indicate to what extent you have felt this way *today*.*

1 = very slightly or not at all; 2 = a little; 3 = moderately; 4 = quite a bit; 5 = extremely.

_____ interested   _____ irritable
_____ distressed   _____ alert
_____ excited   _____ ashamed

(Continued)

____ upset	____ inspired
____ strong	____ nervous
____ guilty	____ determined
____ scared	____ attentive
____ hostile	____ jittery
____ enthusiastic	____ active
____ proud	____ afraid

* The PANAS can also be used with the following time instructions:

Indicate to what extent:

- you feel this way *right now*, that is at the present moment;
- you have felt this way during *the past few days*;
- you have felt this way during *the past week*;
- you have felt this way during *the past few weeks*;
- you have felt this way during *the past year*;
- you *generally* feel this way, that is, how you feel on average.

It is possible that there are no scales available that directly measure what the social psychologist is interested in, for example, a scale on attitudes toward terrorism. In this case, psychologists must develop their own scale based on a careful problem analysis. Constructing a reliable scale is not as easy as it seems. However, this book is not the place to discuss the way to construct a reliable scale. To learn more about scale construction, you may have to take an (advanced) course in methodology and/or read a good book about scale construction (see, for example, *Introduction to test construction in the social and behavioural sciences: A practical guide*, by Fishman & Galguera, 2003).

Box 4.5   The Test Phase: Developing and Testing a Process Model

Developing an empirically based process model includes the following steps:

1. Develop a process model and work your way from the outcome variable on the right to the causal variables on the left; picture the process model in a diagram.
2. Determine whether a particular variable has a direct, indirect, reinforcing or undermining effect on the outcome variable.
3. Limit the number of boxes (variables) in the model to about 10.
4. Don't take more than four steps back in the model.
5. Determine the direction of the relationship between two variables by using + or − signs.
6. Use, as much as possible, concrete and continuous variables.
7. Determine the empirical relationships between variables either by reviewing the empirical literature or by doing your own research.

SUGGESTED FURTHER READING

Albarracín, D., Johnson, B.T. & Fishbein, M. (2001). Theories of reasoned action and planned behaviour as models of condom use: A meta-analysis. *Psychological Bulletin*, *127(1)*, 142–161.

Buunk, B.P. & Schaufeli, W.B. (1999). Reciprocity in interpersonal relationships: An evolutionary perspective on its importance for health. In W. Stroebe & M. Hewstone (Eds.), *European Review of Social Psychology (Vol. 10*, pp. 260–291).

Fishman, J.A. & Galguera, T. (2003). *Introduction to test construction in the social and behavioural sciences: A practical guide*. Lanham: Rowman & Littlefield.

Van Vugt, M. (1998). The conflicts of modern society. *Psychologist, 11(6)*, 289–292.

ASSIGNMENT 4

(a) Make a list of the variables you selected in Assignment 3 (Chapter 3) and develop a process model. Remember to:

- Work your way from the outcome variable on the right to the causal variables on the left.
- Ask yourself whether each variable has a direct, indirect, reinforcing or undermining effect on the outcome variable, and determine the direction of the relationship between two variables by using + or − signs.
- Ensure that you limit the number of variables to about 10 and don't take more than four steps back in the model.
- Ensure that the model does not consist of two or more separate processes.

(b) Read the following articles in detail and examine the empirical validity of the relationships in the process model. If necessary, examine what causes have to be added to the model.

Caughlin, J.P. & Huston, T.L. (2002). A contextual analysis of the association between demand/withdraw and marital satisfaction. *Personal Relationships*, *9(1)*, 95–119.

Caughlin, J.P. & Vangelisti, A.L. (2000). An individual difference explanation of why married couples engage in the demand/withdraw pattern of conflict. *Journal of Social and Personal Relationships*, *17(4–5)*, 523–551.

CHAPTER 5

THE HELP PHASE: DEVELOPING THE INTERVENTION

With Arie Dijkstra

Contents

The Help Phase: Developing the Intervention

INTRODUCTION

Once the factors causing the outcome variable have been identified and mapped in the process model, the intervention can be developed. An intervention is a means to change the causal factors and thus the outcome variables in the desired direction. An adequate intervention targets one or more causal factors in the process model. Yet often it is not feasible or even necessary to target all variables in this model. Therefore, the first step in the Help stage of the PATH model is to determine which causal factors will be targeted in the intervention. The modifiability of the factors and the expected effect sizes of interventions will direct this choice. Once these factors have been identified, an intervention that targets these factors can be developed. Decisions must be made about how the target group will be reached and what the content of the intervention will be. The content depends largely on empirical evidence. The last step in the Help phase concerns the implementation process. Here care is taken that the intervention is used as intended. We want to emphasize that the present chapter only gives an introduction into the art of intervention development, and that more detailed approaches are available elsewhere, for instance, in the context of health education (see for example, Bartholomew, Parcel, Kok & Gottlieb, 2006).

Box 5.1   Case Study: Racial Discrimination and Blood Pressure

It is known that racial discrimination may have severe psychological consequences for people who are discriminated against: they may feel unfairly treated, depressed, angry and/or sad. But can racial discrimination also harm physical health? In general Black US citizens suffer from higher blood pressure than White US citizens. Is it possible that this has something to do with racial discrimination? To answer this question, researchers Nancy Krieger and Stephen Sidney conducted a study* among more than 4000 Black and White adults. Participants' blood pressure was assessed, and they were asked about their experiences with racial discrimination and their ways of coping with it. They were asked, for example, 'Do you accept racial discrimination as a fact of life or do you try to do something about it?', and 'Do you talk to other people about being discriminated against or do you keep it to yourself?'.

The researchers discovered that, surprisingly, among working-class Black men and women, blood pressure was elevated among those who reported either a great deal of racial discrimination or *no* discrimination at all. According to the researchers this does not mean that (intermediate) levels of racial discrimination are healthy. It is, for instance, possible that people who experience discrimination find it too painful to admit to and, consequently, do not report it as such. It is also possible that discriminated individuals suffer from so-called 'internalized oppression', that is, they perceive unfair treatment as 'deserved' and non-discriminatory.

Furthermore, the researchers found that the way Black individuals cope with racial discrimination is at least as important as racial discrimination itself. Among working-class Black men and women blood pressure was highest among those who responded to unfair treatment by accepting it as a fact of life, and did nothing about it.

Krieger and Sidney's (1996) study underlines that racial discrimination is not just a problem for those who are discriminated against, but for society as a whole. Having high blood pressure and falling ill as a consequence of feeling discriminated against may lead to job absenteeism, a loss of productivity and a rise in health-care costs. Moreover, the study suggests that, in addition to anti-discrimination policies aiming to prevent discrimination, the government might also develop a campaign to encourage Blacks not to accept discrimination as a fact of life but to become assertive and to claim their right to fair treatment.

* Krieger, N. & Sidney, S. (1996). Racial discrimination and blood pressure: the CARDIA study of young black and white adults. *American Journal of Public Health, 86*, 1370–1378.

PREPARING INTERVENTION DEVELOPMENT

The essence of the final Help phase is that interventions must focus on changing factors in the explanatory model. It is not always necessary, appropriate, or possible to target all the factors in the explanatory model. Therefore, the applied social psychologist chooses the factors that are *modifiable* and that have the greatest *effect* on the outcome variable. To do so, it is convenient to put all the factors from the process model into a *balance table* (see Table 5.1).

Modifiability

Although presumably many variables in the selected process model can be influenced, there may be considerable differences in the degree to which this is possible. Three questions can help to exclude factors that are difficult to change:

1. Does the factor concern a stable *personality trait*? For example, when a psychologist wants to develop an intervention to tackle shyness, one may include introversion as a personality variable with a high degree of explanatory power in the model, but this variable has little potential for change outside intensive psychotherapy. Or when one includes neuroticism as a variable in a model predicting burnout, one needs to realize that this is a stable personality trait that will be difficult to change.
2. Is the factor related to deeply held *political or religious values*? For example, it will be virtually impossible to attract attention for a programme on condom use from people who, based on their religious convictions, are strongly against premarital sex. Or it may be difficult to convince selection officers with very negative attitudes towards immigrants to endorse a policy to employ people from minority groups.
3. Is the factor related to *stable environmental conditions*? For example, a problem might be that students do not park their bikes in the appropriate parking spaces at university. Perhaps they see many other bikes parked in inappropriate spaces and follow that example. However, this might be due to insufficient bike storage facilities on campus, which is a stable environmental condition.

Effect Size

Not all factors in the process model have an equally strong impact on the outcome variable, and applied psychologists should focus on the ones that have the strongest effect. This selection is facilitated if there is empirical evidence for the strength of the causal relationships in the model. Often, however, this is not available and psychologists 'guestimate' the effect sizes. Various sources of information can be helpful to estimate the effects.

Past Experience with Similar Situations

Suppose a school aims to tackle cultural segregation among their students. In the process model, the recruited psychologist identifies 'knowledge about people from other cultures' and 'personal contact with people from other cultures' as factors predicting segregation. Yet last year the school board decided to provide youngsters with positive knowledge on other cultures, and, although students were more positive, this seemed to have no effect on social interactions in the school. Armed with this knowledge, it does not seem very sensible to try this strategy again.

Empirical Evidence

For a number of factors in the model, there may be empirical evidence that they are resilient to change. For example, the literature shows that most people are unrealistically optimistic about their lives (Weinstein & Klein, 1996). Most children, for example, believe they have less risk than the average child of becoming overweight and developing health problems as a result of being overweight. As this optimism is a statistical impossibility – it simply cannot be that most people are better off than the average person – a psychologist may believe it could help to educate people about this illusion. However, research suggests that such biased perceptions are hard to correct and that their influence on behaviour is limited (Weinstein, 2003). Thus, one would not select this factor to be targeted in an intervention. In general, it makes sense to look for evidence showing the degree to which the model variables are changeable.

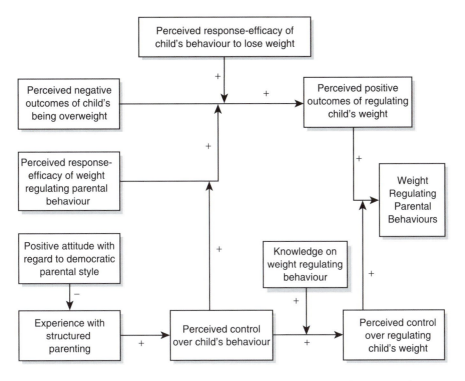

Figure 5.1   Process model: What factors influence weight regulating parental behaviours?

The Balance Table

A balance table helps in making the decision on which factors will be targeted in the intervention. We illustrate the balance table through the problem of obesity among children in the UK. Britain is one of the 'fattest' nations in Europe. In 2000, 27 per cent of girls and 20 per cent of boys aged 2 to 19 years were overweight (see the websites on NationalStatistics, www.statistics.gov.uk). Obesity amongst children is a problem of great concern: such children have a high risk of developing long-term chronic conditions, including adult-onset diabetes, coronary heart disease, orthopaedic disorders, and respiratory disease. A social psychologist is asked to develop an intervention to help tackle this problem. In studying the literature she discovers that one of the major causes of obesity is the influence of parents on the weight of their children (Jackson, Mannix & Faga, 2005), namely, that parents may not do enough to stop weight gain in their children. Such behaviours are referred to as *weight regulating parental behaviours*. A psychologist will develop a process model in which these behaviours are the outcome variable (see Figure 5.1).

Next, a psychologist will evaluate all the variables from the process model with regard to their modifiability and their effect size, that is the magnitude of the impact of the change on the outcome variable.

Table 5.1   Balance table

Variables from the process model	Modifiability	Effect size
1. Perceived negative outcomes of child being overweight	++	+
2. Perceived positive outcomes of weight reducing parental behaviours	++	+
3. Perceived response-efficacy of child's behaviour to lose weight (does a change in the child's behaviour lead to losing weight?)	++	+
4. Perceived control over weight reducing parental behaviours	+	+
5. Knowledge on weight reducing parental behaviours	++	++
6. Perceived control over child's behaviour	+	++
7. Experience with structured parenting	0	+
8. Positive attitude with regard to democratic parental style	0	0 or +

Note   With regard to modifiability: ++ = high modifiable; + = medium modifiable; 0 = low modifiable, – – = not modifiable, +/0 = depends on another variable.
With regard to the effect size: ++ = large effect; + = moderate effect; 0 = small effect; – – = no effect; +/0 = depends on another variable.

First, she evaluates the *modifiability* of the eight causal factors in the process model. The first three factors – the perceived negative outcomes of a child being overweight, the perceived positive outcomes of regulating one's child's weight, the perceived response-efficacy of a child's behaviour to lose weight – are beliefs based on factual knowledge and on interpretations of past events or experiences. In general, beliefs can be influenced quite well. Furthermore, the perceived positive outcomes of weight regulating parental behaviours can only be brought about under conditions of sufficient response-efficacy regarding the child's behaviour, that is, when the parental behaviours produce the desired change in the child's behaviour. The knowledge about weight regulating parental behaviour, and how to perform it, can also be modified as it only requires adequate basic information processing and storage. Structured parenting refers to a parenting style in which children are actively guided and given clear directions for choices and behaviours, for example, concerning food intake and physical exercise. The experience with this type of parenting is also modifiable and can be changed by practising it. Structured parenting is less likely the more parents tend to engage in a democratic parenting style, i.e. have a parenting style in which children are stimulated (or often just left) to make their own choices. A positive attitude with regard to a democratic parental style is perhaps difficult to change as it may be based on parental modelling and a history of perceived **reinforcement** of that style. The conclusions with regard to the factors' modifiability are depicted in Table 5.1.

KT

Next, she will evaluate the *effect size* of the causal factors in the process model. How strong is the effect on the outcome variable? Changes in the first three variables in the balance table are probably possible but their effects on the outcome variable largely depend on parents' perceived control over regulating their children's weight. Just changing these variables may have a small effect as only some parents will have sufficient control beliefs. Changing the knowledge on weight regulating parental behaviour can have a large effect, as it is a primary condition to engage in such behaviour. Changing the positive attitude with regard to a democratic parental style has uncertain effects, as it does not guarantee that an adequate alternative style will be adopted. Changing the perceived control over the child's behaviour can have large effects as it is a basis for developing perceived positive outcomes of regulating the weight of one's children *and* perceived control over this behaviour. Finally, experience with structured parenting can have various effects but it does not guarantee that parents are skilled in the specific behaviours regulating the weight of their children. A psychologist will summarize her findings in the balance table (see Table 5.1).

From the balance table it appears that an intervention that targets the knowledge on weight regulating parental behaviour and the perceived control over a child's behaviour will probably be most successful. In addition, a psychologist may also target the perceived negative outcomes of a child being overweight, the perceived positive outcomes of the parental behaviour, or the perceived response-efficacy of a child's behaviours.

DEVELOPING THE INTERVENTION

Once the psychologist has decided which variables to target, the intervention can be developed. Three tasks can be distinguished in the development of an intervention:

1. Choosing the right *channel*; in which way one may reach the target group members for example.
2. Selecting the appropriate *methods*; the way the changes will be brought about, for example, by offering a role model or performing a skill exercise.
3. Developing the *strategies*; the translation of the methods into concrete aspects of the intervention. For example, when the method is social **modelling**, the strategy refers to the exact model and the things the model says and does.

The channel, the method and the strategy must consider the target group for intervention. A social psychologist may focus on improving patient skill in taking a specific medicine when the target group consists of those patients who already use, or who will use, that particular medicine. The choice of channel is guided by the need to reach this target group (for example, through using a pharmacy) and by the method (for example, modelling: watching another patient taking the medicine on a DVD). The specific model (strategy) demonstrating the skills depends upon the target group (for example, using an older model when the patients are elderly). It is important to note that the development of an intervention is usually a dynamic process: choices for the channel, the method and the strategy are made in combination (see Figure 5.2).

The Channel

The channel is the means through which people are reached and the intended changes will only take place if people are exposed to the channel. In Table 5.2 an overview is

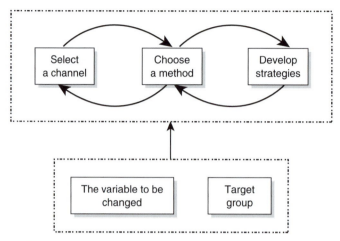

Figure 5.2   The development of an intervention: channel, method and strategy

given of various channels and their characteristics. Channels have several *features*, and may vary from simple (for example, sticker or label) to complex (for example, community intervention), each communicating a distinct type of information (for example, text, picture) and a different volume of information (for example, one simple message versus a complex set of arguments). Some channels communicate with high intensity (say, group therapy) and others with low intensity (say, information signs).

Channels also differ in the potential *reach* of the target group (see Table 5.2). For example, a label on a product has the potential to reach all the users of a product, while a radio message reaches only part of the population of users. In addition, some channels will only have small *effects* on the individual level (say, a sticker), while others can have large effects (the example of group therapy). Lastly, channels may bring about different *types* of effects. For example, a label is appropriate to increase people's knowledge, while counselling is more appropriate to change complex and deeply rooted behaviours.

The channel is chosen on the basis of information about the target group, the relevant variables, methods and strategies. The following issues should be considered when choosing the channel:

1. Is the channel an *effective way* to reach the target group? (See Table 5.3, potential reach.) When people want to know how to use a product, say a wrist-exercise tool, using the label on the tool works better than a television ad. The label ensures that people who buy the tool have access to the information.
2. Is exposure through this channel *intensive enough* to change the variable? (See Table 5.2, effect on individual level.) A billboard depicting a young woman during a physical work-out may remind people that physical exercise is desired, but may not lead to a change in attitudes toward working-out. Daily feedback through the internet, however, may shape people's positive experiences with fitness, leading to the desired changes.

Table 5.2 Overview of various channels and their characteristics

Channel	Features	Potential reach	Effect on individual level	Effect type
• Label	Short informative text on the use of a product delivered with the product	People who buy the specific product	Small	New knowledge
• Information sign/prompt	Simple message relevant in the specific situation, e.g., using arrows, pictograms or core statements	People who encounter the situation	Small	Reminder/Behavioural change
• Sticker	Simple message with relevance not limited to the specific situation	Depends on the application[1]	Small	Reminder
• Billboard	A big sized (e.g., 1 or more square metres) picture, drawing, text or combination	People who pass the billboard	Small	Reminder
• Leaflet	A few pages of information, often illustrated	People who encounter the distribution point	Small	New knowledge/ Psychological change
• Self-help book	Including information, testimonials, psychological tests, exercises etc.	People who visit the bookstore	Medium	New knowledge/ Psychological change
• Magazine	*Vogue, MEN, Time, Cooking Light*, etc.	People who buy the magazine	Small	New knowledge/ Psychological change

Table 5.2 (Continued)

• CD-Rom/DVD	Text, pictures, sound, video, interaction	Depends on the application[2]	Medium	New knowledge/ Psychological change/ Behavioural change
• Internet/E-mail	Information sites, interactive sites, reminder mails, etc	People with access to the internet	Small	New knowledge/ Psychological/ change Behavioural change
• Cell-phone	Reminder calls, SMS	People in the database or all those who request the service	Small	Psychological change/ Behavioural change/Reminder
• Television	Commercials, infomercials, documentaries, spots, etc	People who watch TV channel at the time of broadcasting	Medium	New knowledge/ Psychological change
• Minimal counselling	A few short personal contacts	People who are referred to it	Medium	Psychological change/ Behavioural change
• Extensive counselling	Several or many personal contacts of about 30-60 minutes	People who are referred to it	Medium/Large	Psychological change/Behavioural change
• Group training	Education and skills training in a group; mostly 1 to 10 meetings	People who are referred to it	Medium/Large	Psychological change/Behavioural change
• Group therapy	Applying therapeutic means to induce change in individuals partly by means of the group; often many meetings	People who are referred to it	Large	Psychological change/Behavioural change

Table 5.2 (Continued)

• Regulations/laws	Agreements about permitted or banned behaviours in more or less specified contexts	Depends on the application[3]	Large	Behavioural change
• Structural environmental changes	Changing the environment to regulate experiences or behaviours, e.g. by regulating the exposure to certain stimuli or the availability of a specific product	People who encounter the specific environment	Large	Behavioural
• Community[4] intervention	Changing peoples' experiences or behaviours by changing the structural and **informational influences** of the community they belong to	Members of the community	Small	New knowledge/ Psychological change/ Behavioural change

[1] Stickers can be used in many different ways. For example, they can be distributed freely and then much depends on those people who encounter the distribution point. Stickers can also be distributed together with product X, exposing only those people who buy that particular product.

[2] A CD-Rom/DVD can be distributed in many ways. For example, they can be actively sent to people who are registered in a database, they may be ordered by those who feel they have a need for it or they can be distributed together with product X.

[3] There are many types of regulations and laws and they may be applied broadly or may only be relevant in specific situations.

[4] Community interventions are a composition of various channels developed to influence the same factors.

KT

3. Is the channel *appropriate* for the method and strategy? A sticker is less appropriate for modelling complex skills, such as learning to lead a healthier lifestyle, while an interactive DVD gives several possibilities for modelling and practising healthy skills. (See Table 5.2, effect type.)

4. What is the *impact* on the population level of an intervention using this channel? The impact of an intervention is determined by its *effectiveness*, that is, the proportion of people who change after being targeted, as well as by the *participation rate*, that is, the percentage of people who eventually participate in the intervention. Consider the development of an intervention to lower alcohol abuse in students. We might choose group counselling as the channel, because it has been shown to be highly effective (Galanter, Hayden, Castañeda & Franco, 2005). For example a psychologist estimates that 20 per cent of students who are exposed to this intervention will show a reduction in alcohol intake. However, few students will participate in such an intervention. Less intensive intervention (for example, computer-individualized persuasive information sent through the internet) may only lead to a 10 per cent reduction and this may be less effective but many more students may participate in the programme. The *impact* of an intervention can now be calculated: it is equal to the intervention's effectiveness *times* the intervention's participation rate. For example, if the participation rate of group counselling is 1 per cent while the participation rate for the computer-individualized persuasive information is 5 per cent, the *impact* on the population level would be 0.002 (20 per cent × 1 per cent) for the group counselling and 0.005 (10 per cent × 5 per cent) for the computer-individualized intervention, making the impact of the latter greater than that of the first.

The Method

Intervention methods also require consideration. Methods are often derived from theoretical frameworks. For example, the **foot-in-the-door** technique (Cialdini & Trost, 1998), according to which people more easily accept a major request after first complying to a minor request, is embedded in the **theory of self-perception** that argues that people adjust their attitudes to their behaviours (Bem, 1972). Such theories are important because they specify the conditions under which the method is most or least likely to be successful. For example, according to **social learning theory**, modelling is most effective when the similarity between model and target individual is high (Bandura, 1986). From the various theories, phenomena and concepts in the Glossary (pp. 136–47) one can often deduce ideas about methods.

Selection of a method depends, first, on consideration of the balance table (see Table 5.1). For each variable, an intervention method must be chosen. Suppose 'attitudes of police officers towards foreigners' and 'communication with foreigners' are the selected variables to improve the treatment of tourists in a city in Spain. *Modelling* might be used to demonstrate communication skills, whereas the method of *argumentation* might target attitude change. Second, selection of a method depends on the extent to which the method 'fits' the variable one aims to change. Whereas some channels can motivate people to show the desired behaviour, they cannot teach them *how* to change it. For example, it is easy to arouse fear in smokers through a 30 second television advertisement, but it is difficult to help them quit smoking using this channel. In contrast, it is often sufficient to remind people of the benefits of a certain behaviour by using a prompt. For example, a sign on an elevator door can prompt people to use the stairs for exercise.

The following methods are frequently used in psychological interventions.

Goal Setting

Setting concrete and specific goals is important. Goals direct people's attention and effort, provide them with expectations, and give the opportunity for feedback on goal accomplishment, thereby regulating motivation. Goal setting changes behaviour by defining goals that people must reach in a given period of time (Locke & Latham, 2002). For instance, as regards being overweight, a goal can be set in terms of weight loss in kilos over a particular time period. Sub-goals can help people work on small, but important, steps in reaching the superordinate goal. For example, in patients who have had a stroke, a goal in the rehabilitation could be: 'After three months I can walk 200 metres by myself'. Many studies support the effectiveness of goal setting. Evans and Hardy (2002) examined the effects of a five-week goal-setting intervention for the rehabilitation of injured athletes. The results showed that a goal-setting intervention fostered adherence and self-efficacy. McCalley and Midden (2002) provided participants with feedback to increase household energy conservation behaviour. They showed that participants who had set goals for themselves eventually saved more energy.

Fear Communication

Fear communication can be effective to motivate certain behaviours. For example, health behaviours, such as using condoms, can be encouraged by graphic information about sexually transmitted diseases (Sutton & Eiser, 1984). An interesting study by Smith and Stutts (2003) compared the effects of a fear appeal showing the cosmetic effects of smoking (unhealthy looking faces) with the effects on one's health (cancer). They found that both fear-appeal conditions effectively reduced smoking. It must be noted that fear communication is only effective (and ethically justified) when it is accompanied by explicit guidelines on how to avert the health threat.

Modelling

Modelling refers to learning through the observation of others. Watching others behave and showing the consequences can teach people to perform a new behaviour (Bandura, 1986). Modelling is useful for all kinds of skills, for example, coping with criticism, cooking meals, and using condoms. In a meta-analysis, Taylor, Russ-Eft and Chan (2005) examined the effects of different types of modelling. Do people learn more when a skill is modeled positively (showing what one should do), negatively (showing what one should not do) or in combination? These psychologists concluded that skill development was greatest when role models were mixed, that is, when they showed what one should as well as what one should not do.

Enactive Learning

The most effective way of learning a skill is to try to accomplish it yourself. This is called enactive learning. In interventions, people can be stimulated to practise a certain skill and evaluate it. For instance, to foster students' interest in science subjects like mathematics, Luzzo and his colleagues (1999) exposed students to either a video presentation of two university graduates discussing how their confidence in maths had increased (so-called vicarious learning) or a maths task providing these students with feedback on their maths skills (enactive learning). The enactive learning condition proved more effective.

Social Comparison

Social comparison – information on how others are doing – may affect one's mood and well-being (Buunk & Gibbons, 2007; Festinger, 1954). For example, in the context of coping with cancer, Bennenbroek et al. (2003) provided cancer patients undergoing chemotherapy with social comparison information to increase the quality of their life. The intervention consisted of a tape recording of fellow patients telling their personal stories about either the treatment procedure, emotions experienced during the treatment, or a tape about the way they tried to cope with the situation. The latter tape especially reduced anxiety over the treatment and improved patients' quality of life.

Implementation Intentions

Implementation intentions are intentions to perform a particular action in a specified situation (Sheeran, Webb & Gollwitzer, 2005). Sometimes people are asked to formulate their implementation intentions. For a person who wants a low fat diet an implementation intention could be: 'When I am at the supermarket I will put the low-fat butter in the shopping trolley', or 'When I am at the party on Friday night and somebody offers me cake, I will decline'. Asking people about their implementation intentions may increase the occurrence of desirable behaviours. Steadman and Quine (2004), for instance, showed that asking participants to write down two lines about performing testicular self-examination led to the desired action. Likewise, Sheeran and Silverman (2003) compared three interventions to promote workplace health and safety and found that asking people to write down their implementation intentions was the most effective.

Reward and Punishment

In general, people repeat behaviours that are followed by a positive experience (reward) while avoiding a negative experience (punishment). In the smoking example, a reward may take the form of a refund for the costs of a smoking cessation course from the health insurance company, if people quit smoking for at least three months. In contrast, the government may punish people for smoking by increasing the price of cigarettes. Furthermore, people can learn to reward or punish themselves. For example, people who succeed in refraining from smoking for a week could treat themselves to a cinema visit. In general, there is much evidence for the effects of punishment and rewards. Punishment of undesirable behaviours (for example, high fines for drunk driving) works best when it is accompanied by rewards for desirable behaviours (for example, praise for staying sober before driving) (Martin & Pear, 2003).

Feedback

Feedback on accomplishments is essential in behavioural change. People losing weight want to know how much weight they have lost. Without feedback people become uncertain and their motivation deteriorates because they do not know whether they have made progress (Kluger & DeNisi, 1998). Brug and his colleagues (1998) provided people with tailored computer feedback on their diet (vegetables, fruit and fat intake) and on dietary changes. Both feedback types appeared to improve dietary habits. Likewise, Dijkstra (2005) showed that a so-called fear appeal to smokers – a single sentence of individual feedback ('It appears you are not aware of the changing societal norms with regard to smoking') – was twice as effective in reducing smoking as no feedback.

Box 5.2   Interview with Professor Gerjo Kok of the University of Maastricht (The Netherlands)

One of the oldest and most prominent application areas of social psychological theory is health. Professor Gerjo Kok is one of the leading scientists in this field.

Gerjo Kok: 'Social psychological processes are very helpful in understanding real life. It helps us understand why, for example, people find it so hard to quit smoking or why they practice unsafe sex, despite the risks involved. Insight into the causes of unhealthy behaviours makes it possible to develop interventions that may help people adopt a healthier lifestyle. In one of our studies we found, for instance, that self-evaluations are of central importance in smoking cessation. Self-evaluations refer to the standards that people have set for themselves. When people meet their standards, they will experience positive self-evaluations. They may feel proud when they succeed in not smoking for a day. In contrast, when people fail to meet their standards, they will experience negative self-evaluations. They may regret the fact that they have started smoking again, or feel fed up with themselves. These self-evaluations are of essential importance in smoking cessation, and intervention programmes that help people to stop smoking should pay attention to them. An intervention programme may, for instance, explicitly point out to people how bad they would feel when they would start smoking again.

'In addition to research on the causes of unhealthy behaviour, we have developed a process protocol, called Intervention Mapping, that provides guidelines and tools for the development of health promotion programmes. In certain ways

(Continued)

the protocol is like this book. It helps social psychologists, health organizations and/or the government to translate social psychological theory and research in actual health programme materials and activities and develop health intervention programmes that are maximally effective. In general I see a great future for applied social psychology. I believe that social psychology will play a growing role in the solution of societal and health problems. Especially with regard to the study of unconscious processes (such as habits), the field of group dynamics, and the study of environmental determinants of behaviour (such as social norms and social control) I expect social psychologists to become (even) more active.'
   Interested in Gerjo Kok's research? Then read, for instance:

Dijkstra, A., De Vries, H., Kok, G. & Roijacker, J. (1999). Self-evaluation and motivation to change: Social cognitive constructs in smoking cessation. *Psychology & Health, 14(4)*, 747–759.
Kok, G., Schaalma, H.P., Ruiter, R.A.C., Brug, J. & van Empelen, P. (2004). Intervention mapping: A protocol for applying health psychology theory to prevention programmes. *Journal of Health Psychology, 9*, 85–98.

The Strategy

Methods have to be translated into a specific strategy. The strategy is the actual intervention people will get exposed to. For example, using *television* as the channel and *modelling* as the method, the strategy would specify the age and gender of the role model. In the case of flu vaccinations for elderly people, the strategy might be a television spot ad in which viewers watch an older woman, with good health, being interviewed in her doctor's waiting room, before having her vaccination.

To come up with strategies, a global intervention plan could be made specifying the methods, channels, target groups, and variables to be changed as identified on the basis of the balance table. Here are some examples:

- Modelling (*method*) on television (*channel*) to motivate women with overweight children (*target group*) to monitor their children's body weight (*variable to be changed*).
- Giving feedback (*method*) through the internet (*channel*) about the length of time youngsters (*target group*) engaged in exercise during the past week to support an increase in their physical stamina (*variable to be changed*).
- Offering arguments (*method*) to motivate quitting smoking (*variable to be changed*) in a self-help book (*channel*) for smokers of all ages (*target group*).
- Repetition (*method*) of the word 'action' in the text of a model (*method*) presented in a leaflet (*channel*), designed to motivate obese people (*target group*) to formulate implementation intentions with regard to reserving a seat with extra space (*variable to be changed*) on international flights.

Next, based on these global intervention descriptions, the social psychologist could select a strategy for intervention. This usually takes place in two phases, a divergent and convergent phase. In the divergent phase, the psychologist lists as many strategies as possible. In the convergent phase, he or she critically evaluates these strategies.

The Divergent Phase: Inventing Strategies

There are various techniques to generate interventions:

- *Direct intervention association*. Ideas for strategies can be based on all kinds of sources, such as what one has seen on television, what makes intuitive sense, what has proven to be effective in the literature or what people have experienced themselves.
- *Direct method approach*. This approach consists of looking at strategies that have been used in similar situations. For example, suppose that the global intervention description is: 'Provide information on the appropriate use of a new type of toothbrush on a label to prevent mouth injury in patients with bad teeth.' A psychologist might then inspect existing labels on toothbrushes. Also labels with regard to other devices that could injure people could be used to generate ideas.
- *Debilitating strategies*. This approach is to come up with strategies that have *undesired* effects on the problem. In the case of the global intervention description: 'Modelling on television to motivate women to monitor their children's weight', the model should probably not be a retired millionaire on his ranch. By generating ideas of what would probably have no or reverse effects, we can learn about what would have an effect, about the relevant dimensions of an effective intervention and about ways to operationalize the strategies.
- *Interviews*. Interviewing people from the target group could generate additional ideas for strategies. With the global intervention description, 'Modelling on television to motivate women to monitor their children's body weight', a woman with young children might be interviewed about her preference for role models that might inspire her. Here is an example of such an interview:

Social psychologist:	'If there was to be an intervention on television in which a person tried to convince you that monitoring your children's body weight is important, what kind of person would you trust most?'
Interviewee:	'I think I would be persuaded most by someone with experience of the problem. It should be a mother but knowing how things are manipulated on television I would need to have proof that she really is a mother with experience.'
Social psychologist:	'Do you have any other ideas about the person and what the person would say that would help you to accept the message?'
Interviewee:	'The mother should be a sensible person, with some education. I think she should also be serious about the topic; after all, it is about the health of your children.'
Social psychologist:	'What kind of person would you trust least?'
Interviewee:	'When I got, one way or another, the impression that they are indirectly trying to sell a commercial product I would immediately stop watching.'

This kind of interview – asking for the desired but also the undesired characteristics – can generate new perspectives and ideas about strategies. From the above, we learn that people might feel they are being manipulated, which should of course be avoided.

- *Insights from theory.* This approach consists of looking at relevant social psychological theories. With regard to the method of goal setting, for instance, the difficulty of the goal is crucial (Strecher, Seijts, Kok, Latham, Glasgow, DeVellis, Meertens & Bulger, 1995). In general, goals stimulate performance when they are difficult and offer a challenge but at the same time are within someone's reach. Losing two pounds in two months might not motivate a person much, because the outcome is not very attractive, but losing 20 pounds in two months might be unrealistic. Thus, in developing strategies, the psychologist should look carefully at what the theory predicts.
- *Insights from research.* This approach consists of looking at relevant social psychological research. For example, research shows that people are less defensive with regard to processing threatening information (for example on cancer risks) when their self-esteem is boosted (Sherman, Nelson & Steele, 2000). Therefore, in developing a fear-appeal we might want to include a *self-esteem boosting* method, for example, asking people to write an essay on the good things they have done recently (Reed & Aspinwall, 1998). Such 'manipulations' are described in the method sections of empirical articles and can provide the social psychologist with creative ideas for strategies.

The Convergent phase: choosing the strategy

The divergent phase often results in a laundry list of strategies. Therefore, a limited number of strategies need to be selected. The choice for a particular strategy or set of strategies must have both a theoretical and empirical basis. First the strategy should take into account the conditions underlying the theory. For example, in the case of *modelling*, the theory specifies that the actual model must be similar or at least relevant to people in the target group (Bandura, 1986). Second, it is preferable that the choice of strategy is based on empirical evidence from either laboratory experiments or field studies. Ideally, evidence ought to be available for the combination of the channel, the method, the strategy, the variable to be changed and the target group. For example, for the global intervention description: 'Modelling on television to motivate women to monitor their children's body weight', the strongest evidence would come from a field experiment in which such an intervention was tested in a specified target group against a control condition. Somewhat weaker evidence would come from testing the intervention video in the laboratory. The stronger the empirical evidence for the intervention, the higher the chances that the intervention will indeed be effective.

Sometimes evidence for the effectiveness of a certain strategy is simply not there. In that case, especially when the costs of an intervention programme are high, we recommend that the effectiveness of a new strategy should first be tested through research.

BUILDING THE INTERVENTION PROGRAMME

Once the final strategies have been chosen, the intervention can be shaped. If this concerns visual materials this will often be done in collaboration with a professional graphic designer who is acquainted with the technological possibilities, such as paper sizes, colour use, lay-out, visual angles, and dynamic effects. Here are some rules of thumb for preparing materials, based on our own experiences:

- Be as specific as possible. In the case of a leaflet, formulate the final arguments, write the introduction, link the arguments, and choose the font size and type. In the case of a video with the method of modelling, write the **script** and include what should be said and done and what should happen in the video.
- In the case of an intervention with several channels (for example, billboards and television spots) or sequential elements (for example, group counselling sessions), all parts must be fine-tuned and a protocol must be written as well as with planning the intervention.
- If professional artists are involved, it should be clear how much influence they can have over the end-product. The communication with professional artists should be highly interactive and several versions may have to be designed by the artist in order to come up with a product.
- The intervention often includes more than one strategy. In principle, *all* aspects of the intervention that can be read, seen or heard should be part of a strategy. Thus, the colours, the sizes, the sounds, the timing, the wording, the movement, the background, the aspects of the background, and the specific shapes should all refer to an identifiable strategy. One way to test this is to point to a single aspect of the intervention and ask: 'What strategy is this part of and what is the method of operationalization?'

Pre-Testing the Intervention

Each planned intervention must be pre-tested. The primary function is to improve the intervention and to avoid major flaws in the design. A pre-test does not necessarily include a behavioural measure. It primarily ensures that the target group will *attend* to the message as well as *understand* the message. For example, to assess if people from the target group attend to the persuasive message, they may be asked: 'Did you find the information interesting?', 'Why did you find it not interesting?', and 'Were you still able to concentrate on the message at the end?' In addition to such general questions, one may add more specific questions. For example, when the social psychologist has chosen a role model who is trying to persuade members of the target group, there may be questions like 'How similar do you feel to the person in the video?', 'How sympathetic do you find the person in the video?', 'Did you believe the person on the video indeed suffers from disease X, which he claims to do?', and 'What aspects of the model should be changed for you to believe the person?'. The format of the pre-test usually includes exposing a few target group members to the preliminary intervention and assessing their reactions. This assessment can be done in different ways.

- *Interview.* This is in general a useful method to pre-test the intervention. One may have interviews with individuals from the target group and ask questions like the ones above. In addition, one may ask more specific questions. For instance, people may be asked to read a leaflet and tell the interviewer about their reactions, how reliable they found the information, how realistic they found it, and what they liked or did not like about the content or layout.

- *Quantitative assessment:* With this type of pre-test, people from the target group answer closed questions about the intervention in a questionnaire. For example, they may be asked to rate the reliability of the source on a 7-point scale (from 'not at all reliable' (1) to 'very reliable' (7)) or they may be asked whether the intervention 'took too much time' , 'was just right' or 'was too short'. With a more experimental paradigm, when one wants for example to use a sticker to indicate the location of the fire-extinguisher in the building, this sticker could be pre-tested by comparing different versions.
- *Recall:* The psychologist may also use a recall task, which assesses which aspects of the intervention people from the target group remember after having being exposed to the intervention. This might give an insight into which strategies have the highest salience. Imagine a billboard depicting a celebrity promoting safe sex, but when individuals from the target group are asked to recall the characteristics of the billboard, half of them only remember the name of the celebrity and not what he or she was promoting. In this case, the salience of the messenger has apparently distorted the message of the intervention.
- *Observation:* People from the target group may also be observed while being exposed to the intervention. For example, in the case of testing a billboard, eye movements may be monitored to track which aspects of the billboard they pay most attention. Likewise, when testing an internet website, the link-choices and the time spent on each page might be monitored.
- *Expert opinions:* For pre-testing the intervention, one may also ask the experts involved in bringing about the effects of the intervention. (For example, in the case of a leaflet to increase treatment adherence a doctor might be asked to give his opinion.) Or a shop-keeper who is supposed to hand out a leaflet to everyone who buys product X may be asked whether he or she thinks people will indeed look at the leaflet.

In general, participants seldom agree completely about an intervention in a pre-test. Therefore, an applied social psychologist must not only look at the pre-test data, but must also consider theoretical aspects as well as empirical evidence that may be relevant. After revisions have been made, the improved intervention can be pre-tested a second time. The final version of the intervention can now be developed and distributed.

IMPLEMENTATION OF THE INTERVENTION

When the intervention has been developed the implementation process can start. The implementation process has one major goal: to ascertain that the intervention is used as intended. Thus, when a psychologist develops an intervention campaign with leaflets and television advertisements, members of the target group must be exposed to these messages. When all members are exposed to the intervention (for example, they have all read the leaflet or have at least seen one television advertisement), the intervention is implemented optimally. Note that implementation is not about the effects of the intervention but about positioning the intervention in such a way that it *can* have its effects.

The core challenge of the implementation phase is that the extent to which the target group is exposed to the intervention depends on the people and organizations that are involved in the distribution of the intervention. For example, with regard to a leaflet

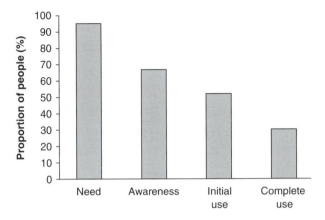

Figure 5.3   Proportion of people who report needing the intervention programme, who are aware of its existence, who have started using it and who have completed the programme

about medicine intake, pharmacists may be involved by motivating their employees to distribute the leaflet to all patients getting a specific medicine. We cannot expect that all these people are as motivated to get the target group members exposed to the intervention as the initiators and developers of the intervention. Therefore, the implementation of an intervention involves motivating others and removing any perceived obstacles to allow them to engage in their specific tasks.

Sometimes people who help with the implementation are simply not aware of the intervention. Paulussen and his colleagues (1995; see also Paulussen, Kok & Schaalma, 1994) studied the implementation of an educational programme consisting of several lessons designed to promote AIDS education in classrooms. Almost all the teachers had initially expressed an interest in participating. Yet only 67 per cent of the teachers were aware of its existence on the curriculum and only 52 per cent initially started to teach it. Although Paulussen et al. (1995) did not assess whether the teachers finished a whole curriculum, this percentage is likely to be substantially lower (see Figure 5.3).

Thus, although psychologists may develop an excellent intervention programme, if only a few people are actually exposed to the intervention because professionals who are essential for its implementation, such as teachers or doctors, are not aware of it or do not use it properly, the impact of the intervention on the problem may be small or non-existent.

The Implementation Process

The implementation process takes time because communication and information exchange take time. Rogers' (1983) model of diffusion of innovations describes how

Figure 5.4 The diffusion process of innovations

large-scale changes in the use of an innovation (for example, using a new toothbrush or using a new method to quit smoking) take place in time. This process is referred to as the *diffusion process*. Rogers distinguishes four phases. We will illustrate the process here with an example of a leaflet for battered women to get professional help. This leaflet is to be handed out by general practitioners if they suspect domestic violence.

1. *Dissemination phase*. In this phase the general practitioner becomes aware of the existence of the leaflet on domestic violence and discusses it with colleagues.
2. *Adoption phase*. In this phase the practitioner becomes motivated to use the innovation and to hand out the leaflet to patients who are suspected to be victims of domestic violence.
3. *Implementation phase*. In this phase the doctor actually engages in the behaviour that will expose the target group to the intervention: he hands out leaflets to the right patients.
4. *Continuation phase*. In this phase handing out the leaflet becomes normal practice.

In stimulating the diffusion process, all four phases will have to be addressed: raising awareness among general practitioners, motivating such practitioners to detect target group members (i.e., women who may be victims of domestic violence), and to hand out the leaflet to these women, supporting the practitioners in the actual execution of the behaviours, and providing feedback and reinforcement to maintain the behaviours (for example, by calling practitioners on the phone and giving them support and advice).

Note that the diffusion process highlights the phases in the implementation process. It does not define all the parties that are involved in the implementation, except for the end users of the innovation (in the above example the general practitioners). The next step is to identify all the people and organizations involved in the implementation process. For each of the four diffusion phases, different people and organizations may be involved.

Mapping the Implementation Route

To be able to organize and optimize the implementation, the implementation route will have to be clear. In the implementation route all the people and organizations that are involved in the implementation and their motivations and barriers to performing their task in the implementation are mapped. Developing an implementation route consists of three steps:

1. *Mapping the actors.* The route shows the actors in the relevant networks in which they communicate and their means of communication. For example, with regard to the implementation of: 'A leaflet with information and arguments for battered women to get professional help', individual general practitioners are members of a regional organization, which is part of the national organization for general practitioners. Within and between these levels of organization, individuals and organizations communicate via different means, including for example, formal meetings, professional journals and email. Furthermore, patients who read the leaflet and decide to seek professional help should be able to make a first appointment very quickly. Thus, the organizations providing professional help to battered women must also be involved in the implementation.
2. *Assessing the motivations and the barriers for actors.* For a successful implementation, each of the actors will have to engage in a specific task. For example, general practitioners should be motivated to engage in detecting battered women and should dedicate some time to this task. Furthermore, the board members of a general practitioners' organization should be motivated to invest some money in persuading general practitioners to perform the detection or to persuade insurers that the detection of battered women should be reimbursed. Thus the implementation route contains for all actors a diagnosis of the potential problems to engaging in the implementation's task and the specific barriers to performing it.
3. *Identifying relevant policies.* Besides identifying the actors involved, the relevant policies also need to be known. For example, it is possible that there is a policy for general practitioners that says that the general practitioner will not engage in detection tasks with regard to family matters. Although some general practitioners might still be motivated, this would not be an ideal situation for the implementation of the intervention. Or it may be that there is a law that says that the police can only offer protection to a battered woman when there is objective evidence of domestic violence. This might inhibit women from seeking professional help. This law would counter the desired effects of the intervention structurally.

The Implementation Plan

When the actors, organizations and policies have been identified and the motivation and the perceived barriers to the actors have been mapped, the implementation plan can be developed. The implementation plan consists of all the steps that should be taken to stimulate the actors to conduct their task(s) in the implementation. In developing an implementation plan, the social psychologist must take two factors into account.

Implementation Goals

For each actor or level of actors and for each of the four diffusion phases, goals may be formulated. For example, a goal for general practitioners in the first diffusion phase could be: '80 per cent of the practitioners heard about the existence of the intervention material on domestic violence and at least 50 per cent discussed the material with colleagues'. On the organizational level, organizational goals should be formulated. For example, a goal in the adoption phase could be: 'The board of the national organization for general practitioners has decided to set aside one article in the professional journal on domestic violence and to develop a pre-publication on it in their communication with the regional organizations'. In principle, the goal should be that every actor has a positive attitude towards the implementation, or perceives their task in the implementation as a legitimate part of their job.

Action Plans

Next, the implementation plan specifies all the actions that must be taken to reach the goals. This implementation manual specifies *how* the goals can be reached. For example, the above goal with regard to the awareness of general practitioners of the intervention materials may be reached by actions directed at their national organization. For example, we might want the board to be motivated enough to decide that some articles on the detection of battered women should be published in their professional journal.

The Actual Implementation

The actual implementation exists through executing the implementation plan. Thus, all kinds of actions will have to be taken to inform and motivate the actors and to take away perceived or actual barriers for actors and to support the implementation. Actors may receive information designed to motivate them, or permission to act from a higher level in their organization or the means, in time or money, to do their part in the implementation. To support the execution of the implementation tasks, the actors might be contacted by e-mail, by letter, by telephone, by advertisements in professional journals, by presentations at meetings or by their internal communication channels.

As may be clear by now, the actual implementation of the intervention is time-consuming and much work has to be done before any target group members will be exposed to it.

The Evaluation

To assess whether the problem that was targeted has indeed changed for the good, the last step in this intervention-development cycle is to evaluate the effects of the intervention. At least three types of evaluation are important: the *effect evaluation*, the *process evaluation* and the *cost-effectiveness evaluation*.

In the *effect evaluation,* the extent to which variables that are directly related to the problem have changed over time is assessed. At the very least the effect of the intervention on the specified outcome variable in the process-model should be assessed. There are, however, more outcome variables that may be evaluated to determine the effectiveness of the intervention. Imagine the case of the problem of obesity in which the level of exercise is the variable that the social psychologist aims to influence. The primary outcome variable in the process model is the level of exercise. However, the number of people who engage in sufficient exercise can also be a meaningful outcome variable. In addition, the percentage of obese people six or 12 months after exposure to the intervention could be an important outcome measure.

To assess to what extent the effects are temporary or permanent, an appropriate follow-up period must be specified. Long-term behavioural effects can be assessed 12 months after the exposure, although the 12 month period is based on consensus rather than on rationale. The best follow-up periods are based on specific arguments for the behaviour that is targeted. For example, because in smoking cessation most smokers who relapse do so within the first six months after the initiation, a six month follow-up should be sufficient; after this period very few ex-smokers relapse.

In the *process evaluation*, the elements that are preconditions for the intervention to be successful are assessed. There are two types of process evaluation. The *primary-process evaluation* refers to an assessment of the changes in the variables that underlie the changes in the outcome variables. For example, when the process model states that prejudice towards Muslims is caused by media misrepresentations of Muslims, the changes in prejudice as a result of unbiased publicity might be assessed in a primary-process evaluation. In principle, all the variables in the balance table that were targeted by the intervention(s) are primary-process variables and may be evaluated. The *secondary-process evaluation* refers to an assessment of the extent to which effective elements of the intervention have indeed been executed. For example, for individual counselling it may be essential that the counselor and the client develop a 'therapeutic relationship' because the therapeutic relationship serves as one of the methods of intervention. In a secondary outcome assessment, the extent to which the therapeutic relationship has been formed is assessed.

In a *cost-effectiveness evaluation* the costs of interventions are assessed and compared with the benefits. For example, obesity has huge societal costs specifically in terms of healthcare provision. If an intervention leads to a yearly decline of 500 people suffering from obesity, the healthcare savings can be calculated. A second aspect of the cost-effectiveness concerns the costs of intervention. The intervention development and implementation are costly as they involve professional labour and material costs. For a television advertisement to be broadcast, the costs for broadcasting must be paid. In the cost-effectiveness evaluation the savings caused by the intervention are compared to the costs of the intervention.

It is important that for the effect evaluation as well as the cost-effectiveness evaluation there are usually data sources available. Many commercial research agencies gather information on societal phenomena, such as the percentage of obese people and the number of unemployed. Thus, it may not always be necessary to gather additional data. On the other hand, it is important that outcome variables are carefully

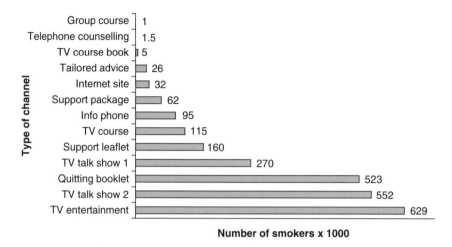

Number of smokers x 1000

Figure 5.5   Number of smokers (x 1000) 'as a function of type of channel' that were reached by the Millennium campaign 'I can do that too'

assessed. Therefore, a self-developed outcome assessment may be necessary. Especially with regard to the process evaluation, reliable measures must often be developed. (For further reading on the evaluation of intervention we would refer to other sources such as *Action evaluation of health programmes and changes* by John Ovretveit, 2001.) In the last paragraphs of this chapter we present a case study of a large-scale intervention that was successfully implemented to help smokers quit in the Netherlands.

Case Study: The Millennium Campaign 'I Can Do That Too'

In the Netherlands, the Dutch Expertise Center of Tobacco Control developed the Millennium campaign 'I can do that too' to reduce the percentage of smokers. The campaign consisted of a series of interventions through several channels to stimulate smokers to quit and support their attempt. The campaign started in October 1999 and ended in February 2000.

The intervention programme is depicted in Figure 5.5. In addition, the population was exposed to free publicity about the campaign. In the written media, no less than 519 articles were published on the Millennium campaign and 79 radio and TV items gave information on it.

The effectiveness of the campaign was assessed using a so-called panel design with measurement control groups (see Box 5.3). That is, before the campaign started, in October 1999 (Time 1), an initial measurement among smokers was conducted. This group constituted the panel group. It is common that such measurements may influence measurements done later with the same group. If one finds a change in the panel group, this could be an artefact of the first measurement (for instance, because it made them aware of the risks of their smoking habits). Therefore, when the second measurement was applied to the panel group (thus at Time 2, in February 2000) there was also a control group of smokers with no Time 1 measurement. The same was done for the Time 3 measurement (January 2001).

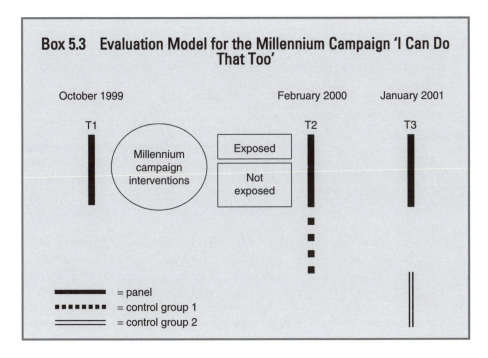

Box 5.3 Evaluation Model for the Millennium Campaign 'I Can Do That Too'

In evaluating the effectiveness of the Millennium campaign, three outcome measures were used:

1. seven-days' abstinence (not smoking for at least the past seven days);
2. having engaged in an attempt to quit;
3. having positive intentions to stop smoking.

It was found that, at Time 2, those smokers who had watched the TV programme or the TV talk show at Time 1 had made significantly more attempts to quit. The long-term follow-up (Time 3) showed that smokers who knew the Millennium campaign also had more positive intentions to stop smoking. The researchers concluded that the Millennium campaign led more smokers to quit smoking and, for those who had not yet made an actual attempt, it had made smoking cessation a higher priority.

> ## Box 5.4   The Help Phase: Developing an Intervention Programme
>
> Developing an intervention programme includes the following steps:
>
> 1. Make a list of all the causal variables in the process model and determine for each of them how modifiable they are and how large their effect will (probably) be. Make a balance table to summarize the results. Choose those factors for your intervention that are modifiable and that have the greatest effect on the outcome variable.
> 2. For each of the selected variables, come up with a channel, a method and a strategy to influence this variable. Justify your choices for the channels and methods and report on the use of different skills to look for appropriate strategies (i.e., direct intervention association, direct method approach, explore debilitating strategies, conduct interviews, look at relevant theories and research).
> 3. Reduce the potential list of strategies. In selecting suitable strategies take notice of the conditions underlying the theory that the particular strategy is based on and look for research that supports the effectiveness of that particular strategy. Develop the strategies you have chosen into an holistic intervention programme.
> 4. Pre-test the intervention programme by means of interviews, quantitative assessments, recall tests or observations.
> 5. Develop an implementation route. Map the actors involved in the intervention's implementation, assess the actors' motivations and the barriers they perceive, and identify relevant policies.
> 6. Develop an implementation plan. What steps have to be taken to mobilize and motivate the actors involved in implementing the intervention?
> 7. Implement the intervention programme and evaluate its effectiveness.

SUGGESTED FURTHER READING

Bartholomew, L.K., Parcel, G.S., Kok, G. & Gottlieb, N.H. (2006). *Planning health promotion programmes: An intervention mapping approach*. San Francisco, CA: Jossey-Bass.

Ovretveit, J. (2001). *Action evaluation of health programmes and changes: A handbook for a user-focused approach*. Abingdon, UK: Radcliffe Publishing.

Rochlen, A.B., McKelley, R.A. & Pituch, K.A. (2006). A preliminary examination of the 'Real Men, Real Depression' campaign. *Psychology of Men & Masculinity, 7(1)*, 1–13.

Smith, K.H. & Stutts, M.A. (2003). Effects of short-term cosmetic versus long-term health fear appeals in anti-smoking advertisements on the smoking behaviour of adolescents. *Journal of Consumer Behaviour, 3(2)*, 157–177.

Van Assema, P., Steenbakkers, M., Stapel, H., Van Keulen, H., Rhonda, G. & Brug, J. (2006). Evaluation of a Dutch public-private partnership to promote healthier diet. *American Journal of Health Promotion, 20(5)*, 309–312.

ASSIGNMENT 5

A company that produces computer software asks you, as a social psychologist, for advice. The company consists of 10 departments, each of 50 employees, with every department managed by an executive. These 10 executives are in turn subordinate to a team of five directors that leads the company. Although 50 per cent of the employees are female, of the directors and executives only one person – the executive that runs the household department – is female. The team of directors asks you how they can improve the upward mobility of women in the company's hierarchy so the company will have more female leaders in the future.

(a) Read the following two articles:
   Ritter, B.A. & Yoder, J.D. (2004). Gender differences in leader emergence persist even for dominant women: An updated confirmation of role congruity theory. *Psychology of Women Quarterly*, *28(3)*, 187–193.
   Eagly, A.H. & Karau, S.J. (2002). Role congruity theory of prejudice toward female leaders. *Psychological Review*, *109(3)*, 573–598.
   Select from these articles causal factors and develop a process model. Make sure that you limit the number of variables to about 10 and don't take more than four steps back in the model.
(b) Estimate for each causal factor in the process model its modifiability and effect size. Make a balance table and select the causal factors at which the intervention should be targeted.
(c) For each of the selected factors, come up with possible strategies to influence this factor. Use direct intervention association and the direct method approach, explore debilitating strategies, conduct interviews, and look at relevant theories and research.
(d) Reduce the potential list of strategies by examining their theoretical and empirical basis.
(e) Outline a global intervention plan, a number of ways to present the intervention and make a plan for the implementation of the intervention.
(f) Develop an evaluation procedure to determine the effectiveness of the intervention programme.

CONCLUSION: LOOKING BACKWARD AND FORWARD

After studying the previous chapters and completing the various exercises, the basic skills for addressing practical problems through applying social psychological theories will have been developed. Nevertheless, it usually takes quite some time and experience before our PATH model can be used in an optimal way. In the beginning you can follow the structured procedures outlined here in a somewhat rigid way. There is nothing wrong with that. On the contrary, this is the best way of learning basic skills and of obtaining experience and a sense of competence. Eventually, however, you will learn that the thing that matters most in the end is to get to a theoretically sound, empirically-based intervention.

Indeed, it is important to be quite flexible in applying the various procedures outlined in this book. The more experience you get, the more likely it is that you can switch between the various steps in the model, and will go back and forth between, for instance, developing a problem formulation and coming up with explanations, or between developing a process model and developing interventions. Gradually, you will become more and more able to 'play' with the procedures, will know when and how to switch between stages, and will develop a sense for when and how to skip a stage. Most people will eventually develop their own approach that deviates from the PATH model, but that has proven its value in practice. In fact, our model has as its main goal allowing social psychologists to develop their own effective approach.

We have said little about how to present the results of one's analyses to the client. This is, however, an important issue. In general, a psychologist should not try to present clients with the outcomes of the various exercises and procedures as they are presented in this book. These exercises and procedures are no more than the tools of the applied psychologist. Just as a carpenter does not reveal all the details of furniture making to his client, but just delivers the end product, a professional who designs interventions for social problems does not present the whole history of the development of the intervention to the client. Usually, he or she would present an analysis of the problem, the major causes that can be addressed in an intervention, and the nature of the intervention. Such a presentation needs to be given in clear and crisp language, without too many scientific terms and without any jargon. Social psychological concepts may be introduced, as far as they clarify the analysis of the problem.

For example, a concept like 'the bystander effect' will be easily understood by an audience and may put a problem in the right perspective. A term like 'self-efficacy' may be necessary when presenting an intervention that is aimed at enhancing the control individuals experience over their situation. But you should not generally describe in detail how you generated your explanations and developed the intervention. Even worse would be to focus your presentation on the explication of social psychological theories, with the help of complex diagrams and schemas. The central goal should be to make clear what you are proposing and to convince a client that this is a well-developed and effective approach.

This implies, among other things, that a psychologist should not constantly bother a client with all kinds of doubts and considerations. There is no need to let clients share in all the deliberations in choosing a given theory or intervention. When you cannot convince yourself, it is unlikely that you can convince others. Of course, a psychologist may explicitly want to present various alternative interventions with their own advantages and disadvantages to give a client various options. But the goal then is to facilitate choice by the client, not to recapitulate the considerations behind your own choice.

To conclude, this book presents an elaborate procedure for developing theory-based interventions, the PATH method. This PATH method is a tool rather than a ritual that one should go through at all costs. It is our belief that social psychological concepts and theories may help in analysing and solving social problems. The goal of this book is to facilitate that and provide those faced with the problem of developing interventions for a variety of social problems with procedures that may help them to accomplish that task.

GLOSSARY

SOCIAL PSYCHOLOGICAL THEORIES, PHENOMENA AND CONCEPTS FOR EXPLAINING SOCIAL PSYCHOLOGICAL PROBLEMS

Theories

affect-infusion model: a model that holds that mood affects the individual's judgment depending on the type of reasoning being used.

arousal: cost-reward model: a model that holds that another person's distress causes physiological arousal in an observer which, in turn, initiates the process of deciding whether to help.

attachment theory: theory about the emotional bond between infants and their caregivers, that assumes that individuals may develop on the basis of the bonds with their caregivers either a secure and avoidant or an anxious-ambivalent attachment style. This attachment style affects one's capacity for relationships in one's adult life, as well as other aspects in one's life, such as one's commitment to work.

attribution theory: a theory that explains the causes of events that happen to one-self or others. The attribution of these causes are known to influence performance affecting reactions etc.

balance theory: a theory that holds that people have an innate preference for a harmonious and consistent relationship among their cognitions.

cognitive dissonance theory: according to this theory people will experience unpleasant psychological tension if they perceive that their cognitions are psychologically inconsistent with their behaviour ('dissonance'). Dissonance will motivate individuals to find ways to reduce it.

complementarity hypothesis: hypothesis that states that persons with dissimilar but compatible traits will be attracted to each other.

contact hypothesis: according to this hypothesis bringing members of different groups into contact with one another will reduce any pre-existing prejudice between them and result in more positive intergroup attitudes and stereotypes.

cultural theories: theories that state that, as individuals engage in particular cultural contexts, their psychologies are shaped accordingly.

elaboration-Likelihood Model (ELM): a model of persuasion that states that people may follow two routes of information processing: the central route (i.e. elaborate issue-relevant arguments) and the peripheral route (i.e. paying attention to peripheral cues such as the attractiveness of the source).

empathy-altruism hypothesis: hypothesis that states that empathy is associated with the selfless desire to benefit another and that empathically-motivated altruistic behaviour is not due to the desire for external rewards, the goal of avoiding guilt, or other selfish desires.

equity theory: a theory that states that people are happiest in relationships where the give-and-take are about equal.

evolutionary psychology: a theory that aims to explain the origins and maintenance of social behaviour from how that behaviour may have contributed to survival and reproductive success in our evolutionary past.

frustration-aggression model: according to this model the interruption of goal-directed behaviour, arising from either the arbitrary interference of other persons or personal inability, evokes frustration which in turn evokes a negative effect and aggressive behavioural tendencies.

general Adaptation Syndrome Model (GASM): a model that presents a three stage reaction to stress (alarm reaction, resistance, exhaustion).

heuristic-Systematic Model: a model of attitude change that specifies two routes to persuasion: systematic processing (i.e. an analytic orientation to information processing) and heuristic processing (i.e. a more restricted mode of information processing that makes fewer demands on cognitive resources).

interdependence theory: a theory that focuses on how individuals weigh the costs and benefits of a particular relationship and how their behaviours are affected by these evaluations. It holds that individuals will be most committed to a relationship when their satisfaction is high, the alternatives for their current relationship are unattractive, and the emotional and practical barriers against leaving the relationship are high.

negative state relief model: according to this model a negative mood is accompanied by a corresponding drive to reduce whatever bad feelings are present. For instance, according to this model a bad mood increases helpfulness because helping another person reduces one's own bad feelings.

norm theory: theory that postulates that every experience brings its own frame of reference or norm into being, either by guiding memory retrieval or by constraining mental simulation.

prospect theory: a theory that describes decisions under uncertainty in which the value of an outcome and its alternatives is calculated as the summed products (n) over specified outcomes (x).

prototype theory: a theory that a category's mental representation is based on a prototypical exemplar or prototype.

rational choice theory: according to this theory, in choosing lines of behaviour, individuals make rational calculations with respect to the utility of alternative lines of conduct, the costs of each alternative in terms of utilities foregone, and the best way to maximize utility.

reinforcement theory: according to this theory reinforcers can control behaviour.

self-affirmation theory: according to this theory people seek information about their own goodness as a human being.

self-categorization theory: a theory that is concerned with the variation in self-categorization in the level, content and meaning of self-categories, and with the antecedents and consequences of such variations. An important variation is self-categorization at the individual or group level (social identity).

self-discrepancy theory: a theory that holds that people are strongly motivated to maintain a sense of consistency between their actual self (how they view they are) and their ideal self (how they want to be), as well as their ought self (how they think they should be).

self-Evaluation Maintenance Model (SEM): a model that holds that self-evaluation depends on three variables in relation to other people: performance, closeness and relevance.

self-perception theory: a theory that holds that people come to know their internal states partially by inferring them from observations of their own overt behaviour and/or the circumstances in which this behaviour occurs.

self-verification theory: a theory that states that individuals seek information consistent with their own self-views, even when that information is negative.

similarity-hypothesis: an hypothesis that states that people are attracted to others who are similar to themselves.

social comparison theory: a theory about individuals' comparisons with other people and the effects of those comparisons on cognitions, effect and behaviours.

social exchange theory: a theory that assumes that how individuals feel about a relationship with another person depends on their perceptions of the balance between what they put into the relationship and what they get out of it.

social identity theory: a theory of group membership, processes and intergroup relations, stating that individuals tend to categorize themselves rapidly as a member of a group, which will lead to favouring one's own group over other groups.

social impact theory: a theory that claims that all forms of social influence will be proportional to a multiplicative function of the strength, immediacy, and number of people who are the source of influence and inversely proportional to the strength, immediacy and number of people being influenced.

social learning theory: a theory that states that people can learn by observing the behaviour of others and the outcomes of those behaviours.

social role theory: according to this theory men and women behave differently in social situations and take different roles, due to the expectations that society puts upon them.

status-expectation states theory: a theory that holds that individuals make judgments about each other on the basis of status characteristics (for example age, ability, gender, race).

subjective expected utility theory: a theory that holds that in choice situations people prefer the option with the highest subjectively expected utility.

theory of planned behaviour: an extension of the theory of reasoned action. This theory adds the concept of 'perceived behavioural control' so that it also becomes possible to predict actions that are under incomplete volitional control.

theory of reasoned action: a theory that aims to predict volitional action and that posits that intentions are the immediate antecedents of behaviour and that these intentions are determined by attitudes towards the behaviour and by the perceived social norms.

transactional model of stress: model that defines stressful experiences as person-environment transactions that depend on the impact of the external stressor and the person's appraisal of the stressor and his or her resources for dealing with the stressor.

triangle hypothesis: hypothesis that asserts that people with a primary competitive orientation expect others also to be competitive, whereas cooperatively oriented individuals expect more variation from others.

Phenomena

actor-observer effect: the phenomenon that actors tend to attribute their actions to situational factors whereas observers tend to attribute the same actions to stable personal dispositions.

buffering effect: the phenomenon that having a particular resource or positive quality protects a person against the adverse impact of a stressful event.

bystander effect: the phenomenon where persons are less likely to intervene in an emergency situation when others are present than when they are alone.

cognitive consistency: the tendency for people to prefer congruence or consistency among their various cognitions, especially their beliefs, values and attitudes.

de-individuation: a state of reduced self-awareness associated with immersion and anonymity within a group.

diffusion of responsibility: the tendency for people to feel that responsibility for acting is shared, or diffused, among those present. That is, the greater the number of people who are present, the lower the individual's sense of responsibility.

distributive justice: the phenomenon that people evaluate the outcomes they receive from others not by their absolute favourability but by their consistency with principles of outcome fairness.

emotional contagion: the tendency to express and feel emotions that are similar to and influenced by those of others.

excitation transfer: the phenomenon that arousal elicited by one stimulus may mistakenly be attributed to another.

false consensus effect: the phenomenon that people tend to perceive their own preferences, attributes or behaviour as more common and situationally appropriate than those of individuals who have alternative preferences, attributes or behaviours.

false uniqueness: a tendency for people to overestimate the uniqueness of their own attributes, which occurs particularly associated for positive attributes.

fundamental attribution error: the tendency for perceivers to underestimate the impact of situational factors and to overestimate the role of dispositional factors in controlling behaviour.

gestalt: a whole which is more than the sum or average of individual elements.

group polarization: a tendency for groups to make decisions that are more extreme than the average of members' initial positions.

groupthink: a mode of thinking that people engage in when they are deeply involved in a cohesive ingroup and that occurs when members' strivings for unanimity override their motivation to realistically appraise alternative courses of action.

halo-effect: phenomenon where a person's positive or negative traits may 'spill over' from one area of their personality to another in others' perceptions of them.

illusion of control: the incorrect perception that a person's actions can affect the outcomes of chance events.

illusory correlation: the perception that two classes of events are correlated which in reality are not correlated or are correlated to a lesser extent than perceived.

illusory superiority: the tendency for people to think they are better and more competent than the 'average' person.

informational influence: the tendency for people to accept information obtained from another as evidence about reality.

just world phenomenon: the phenomenon that people tend to see the world as a just place that leads them to perceive that people receive the outcomes they deserve, especially negative outcomes such as accidents and diseases.

mere exposure effect: the phenomenon that repeated, unreinforced exposure to a stimulus results in increased liking for that stimulus.

misattribution of arousal: the incorrect attribution of arousal to a cause other than the actual one.

negativity effects: the enhanced impact of negative information (relative to positive information) on human functioning.

normative influence: the tendency for people to conform to the positive expectations of others, motivated by the desire for approval and to avoid rejection.

outgroup homogeneity: the phenomenon that members of a group are seen as more homogeneous and similar to one another by an outgroup relative to ingroup members' perceptions.

positive illusion: the tendency for people to unrealistically assess their abilities.

primacy effect: the phenomenon that impressions are influenced more by early rather than later information about a person.

procedural justice: the phenomenon that, when evaluating their outcomes with others, people judge the fairness of the procedures by which those outcomes were determined.

recency-effect: the phenomenon that later information supplants earlier information. Occurs when the impression concerns an unstable attribute, or when attention is focused on later information.

risky shift: the phenomenon that a group which already favours risk to some extent, reaches, through group discussion, a group decision that is even more risky.

self-fulfilling prophecy: the phenomenon that an originally false social belief leads to its own fulfillment.

self-serving bias: the tendency for people to attribute their successes to internal causes such as ability and their failures to external causes such as task difficulty.

social dilemma: a situation in which people's self-interest is at odds with the collective interest.

social facilitation: the phenomenon that an individual's performance may be facilitated by the presence of either passive audiences or other persons performing the same task.

social loafing: the tendency for individuals to exert less effort on a task when working for a group than when working for themselves.

Concepts

affect: a general term describing mental processes that involve feeling, such as an emotional experience or mood.

altruism: a type of helping behaviour with the primary goal of reducing another person's distress.

arousal: an organism's level of physiological activation or excitation.

associative network: a model of human memory as the connections among isolated items of stored knowledge.

attention: whatever occupies consciousness/a person's mental focus at a particular time.

attitude: a psychological tendency that is expressed by evaluating a particular entity with some degree of favour or disfavour.

authoritarianism: an orientation which is overly deferential to those in authority whilst simultaneously adopting an overbearing and hostile attitude towards those perceived as inferior.

automaticity: information processing that occurs without conscious control.

bogus pipeline: a procedure intended to reduce distortions in self-report measures by convincing participants that the researcher has a valid and reliable means of knowing what their true responses are.

categorization: the process of classifying things or people as members of a group or category, similar to other members of that group or category and different from members of other groups or categories.

cognition: mental functions such as the ability to think, reason, and remember.

collectivism (vs. individualism): circumstances in which the meaning of a person and its realization are expressed predominantly in relationships.

cognitive appraisal: a mental process by which people assess whether a demand threatens their well-being and whether they have the resources to meet this demand.

commitment: the binding of an individual to a specific line of activity/ or relationship.

comparison level (Cl): an internal standard representing the quality of outcomes an individual expects to obtain in a relationship.

comparison level of alternatives (Clalt): an internal standard representing the quality of outcomes an individual perceives to be available outside of the current relationship.

construct validity: the extent to which the measured variables accurately capture the constructs of theoretical interest.

counterfactual thinking: the thoughts people have about the alternative ways in which an event could have occurred.

descriptive norms: perceptions of how other people are actually behaving, whether or not this is approved of.

door-in-the-face: technique that obtains compliance to the target request by first obtaining non-compliance to a larger request.

drive: a person's internal state that energizes and maintains behaviour.

ego-involvement: the extent to which a task or issue is personally significant or motivating to an individual, and hence carries implications for that individual's self-concept or self-esteem.

experiment: a type of research in which a researcher randomly assigns people to two or more conditions, varies the treatments that people in each condition are given, and then measures the effect on some response.

external validity: the extent to which one can generalize from one particular setting to another.

foot-in-the-door: technique that predisposes people to comply to a critical request by first obtaining compliance to a minor request.

gender difference: differences between females and males (also called sex-difference).

gender identity: individuals' subjective feeling of themselves as males or females.

gender roles: the socially assigned roles traditionally associated with each sex.

gender stereotypes: beliefs about the behaviours and characteristics of each sex.

helping behaviour: voluntary acts performed with the intent of providing benefit to another person.

heuristic: a cognitive structure or process that serves the creative function of knowledge enrichment and productive thinking.

internal validity: the extent to which the research permits causal inferences about the effects of one variable upon another.

implicit personality theories: tacit assumptions regarding people's personality traits and the relationships among them.

impression formation: the process of forming evaluative and descriptive judgments about a target person.

impression management: the goal-directed activity of controlling or regulating information in order to influence the impression formed by an audience.

individualism (vs. collectivism): circumstances in which the worth of a person is predominantly defined as independent of the membership of groups.

injunctive norms: norms that state the ideal behaviour and that reflect basic values.

intrinsic motivation: form of motivation produced by the experience of free choice and autonomy.

locus of control: an individual's generalized expectancies regarding the forces, internal or external, that determine rewards and punishments.

loneliness: the unpleasant experience that occurs when a person's network of social relationships is deficient in some important way, either quantitatively or qualitatively.

memory: mechanisms by which people store and retrieve the knowledge they have encoded.

meta-analysis: the statistical integration of the results of independent studies in a specific area of research.

minimal group paradigm: research in which anonymous participants are experimentally classified as members of ad hoc, arbitrary or minimally meaningful categories (e.g. X vs. Y) and respond to non-identifiable members of their own and other categories.

minority social influence: a form of social influence in which a deviant subgroup rejects the established norm of the majority of group members and induces the majority to move to the position of the minority.

modelling: a process in which human thought, affect and action are altered by observing the behaviour of others and the outcomes they experience.

mood: generalized positive or negative feeling states.

nonverbal communication: the transmission of information and influence by an individual's physical and behavioural cues.

path analysis: the analysis of data to estimate the coefficients of a class of hypothesized causal models.

personality: intrinsic human qualities that lead to differences among individuals in their characteristic patterns of behaviour.

personal space: the distances and angles of orientation that people maintain for one another as they interact.

person perception: the detection of people's 'internal' psychological qualities, such as abilities, emotions, beliefs and goals.

prejudice: the holding of derogatory attitudes or beliefs, the expression of negative affect or the display of hostile or discriminatory behaviour towards members of a group on account of their membership within that group.

priming: the activation of particular connections or associations in memory just before carrying out an action or task.

prisoner's dilemma: a mixed-motive reward structure in which each of two or more parties must choose between cooperation and non-cooperation.

prosocial behaviour: a broad category of interpersonal actions that are positively evaluated with reference to cultural or societal standards.

prototype: the most typical member of a category.

reactance: a motivational state in response to influence attempts from others, directed towards the reestablishment of one's behavioural freedoms.

reciprocity: responding to the positive or negative actions of others in a similar way.

reference group: any group that individuals use as a basis for social comparison.

reinforcer: any stimulus that, when contingent on a response, serves to increase the rate of responding.

relative deprivation: a psychological state in which there is a perceived negative discrepancy between one's current situation and that which was expected or that which is felt as deserved.

salience: a property of a stimulus that causes it to stand out and attract attention.

schema: cognitive structures that represent a person's knowledge about an object, person or situation, including information about attributes and relationships among those attributes.

script: a schema that describes the typical sequence of events in a common situation.

self-appraisal: the process of seeking, in a relatively impartial manner, information that facilitates an accurate assessment about (aspects of) oneself.

self-awareness: a state in which the person is the object of his/her own attention.

self-concept: the composite of ideas, feelings and attitudes that a person has about his/her own identity, worth, capabilities and limitations.

self-disclosure: the process by which individuals reveal their innermost feelings and experiences to interaction partners.

self-efficacy: people's belief about their capability to produce performances that influence events affecting their lives.

self-enhancement: the process of interpreting and explaining information in such a way that has favourable or flattering implications for oneself.

self-esteem: a positive evaluation of oneself (also called feelings of self-worth or self-respect).

self-handicapping: the act of creating or inventing an obstacle to one's performance in order to avoid looking incompetent.

self-monitoring: individual differences in the extent to which people monitor (i.e. observe and control) their expressive behaviour and self-presentation.

self-presentation: the conscious or unconscious attempt to control images of the self that are conveyed to audiences during social interactions.

social categories: categories individuals use to interpret the social world.

social categorization: the process of assigning a target person to an existing social category.

social cognition: name for both a branch of psychology that studies the cognitive processes involved in social interaction, and an umbrella term for these processes themselves.

social comparison: the process of comparing an ability, opinion or characteristic of one's self to that of another person.

social comparison orientation: individual differences in the extent to which people compare themselves with others.

socialization: the process whereby people acquire the rules of behaviour and the systems of beliefs and attitudes that will equip a person to function effectively as a member of a particular society.

social norm: generally accepted way of thinking, feeling or behaving that is endorsed and expected because it is perceived as the right and proper approach.

social support: the existence of positive social relationships that may help maintain or advance one's health and well-being.

social value orientation: individual differences in the utility derived from outcomes for others. Three types are distinguished: a prosocial orientation, an individualistic orientation, and a competitive orientation.

stereotypes: societally shared beliefs about the characteristics that are perceived to be true of social groups and their members.

stereotyping: the use of stereotypes when judging others.

stress: people's physiological or psychological response to demands from the environment that either approach or exceed their capacities to respond.

subjective expected utility (SEU): the probability of an outcome times the utility of that outcome.

survey: systematic data collection about a sample drawn from a larger population.

trait: a stable, internal property that distinguishes among individuals.

transactive memory: a system shared among group members for encoding, storing and retrieving information such that detailed memories are available to group members without actual physical possession.

type A behaviour: behavioural attributes that increase the risk of coronary heart disease, such as striving for achievement, competitiveness, impatience, and hostility.

unconscious processes: mental processes that occur without awareness.

unobtrusive measure: a non-reactive form of data collection (i.e. it does not require the cooperation of participants).

values: trans-situational goals that serve as guiding principles in the life of a person or group.

BIBLIOGRAPHY

Abrams, D. & Hogg, M.A. (2004). Meta-theory: Lessons from social identity research. *Personality and Social Psychology Review, 8(2)*, 98–106.

Adih, W.K. & Alexander, C.S. (1999). Determinants of condom use to prevent HIV infection among youth in Ghana. *Journal of Adolescent Health, 24(1)*, 63–72.

Ajzen, I. (1987). Attitudes, traits and actions: Dispositional predictions of behavior in personality and social psychology. In L. Berkowitz (Ed.), *Advances in Experimental Social Psychology* (Vol. 20, pp. 1–63). New York: Academic Press.

Ajzen, I. (1991). The theory of planned behavior. *Organizational Behavior and Human Decision Processes, 50(2)*, 179–211.

Ajzen, I. & Fishbein, M. (2000). The prediction of behaviour from attitudinal and normative variables. In T.E. Higgins & A.W. Kruglanski (Eds.), *Motivational science: Social and personality perspectives* (pp. 177–190). New York: Psychology Press.

Albarracín, D., Johnson, B.T. & Fishbein, M. (2001). Theories of reasoned action and planned behaviour as models of condom use: A meta-analysis. *Psychological Bulletin, 127(1)*, 142–161.

Aronson, E., Wilson, T.D. & Akert, R.M. (2002). *Social psychology* (4th edn). Upper Saddle River, NJ: Prentice-Hall.

Bales, R.F. & Cohen, S.P. (1979). *SYMLOG: A system for the multiple level observation of small groups*. New York: Free Press.

Bandura, A. (1986). *Social foundations of thought and action: A social cognitive theory*. Englewood Cliffs, NJ: Prentice-Hall.

Bargh, J.A., Chen, M. & Burrows, L. (1996). Automaticity of social behaviour: Direct effects of trait construct and stereotype activation on action. *Journal of Personality and Social Psychology, 71(2)*, 230–244.

Bartholomew, L.K., Parcel, G.S., Kok, G. & Gottlieb, N.H. (2006). *Planning health promotion programs: An intervention mapping approach*. San Francisco, CA: Jossey-Bass.

Batson, D.C. (1991). *The altruism question: Toward a social-psychological answer*. Hillsdale, NJ: Erlbaum Associates.

Batson, D.C. & Powell, A.A. (2003). Altruism and prosocial behaviour. In T. Millon & M.J. Lerner (Eds.), *Handbook of psychology: Personality and social psychology* (Vol. 5, pp. 463–484). Hoboken, NJ: John Wiley & Sons.

Baumeister, R.F. (1999). *The self in social psychology*. New York: Psychology Press.

Baumeister, R.F. & Tice, D.T. (1990). Anxiety and social exclusion. *Journal of Social and Clinical Psychology, 9*, 165–95.

Bazerman, M.H., Curhan, J.R., Moore, D.A. & Valley, K. (2000). Negotiation. *Annual Review of Psychology, 51*, 279–314.

Becker, R. & Mehlkop, G. (2006). Social class and delinquency: An empirical utilization of rational choice theory with cross-sectional data of 1990 and 2000 German General Population Surveys (Allbus). *Rationality and Society, 18(2)*, 193–235.

Bell, P.A. & Baron, R.A. (1974). Environmental influences on attraction: Effects of heat, attitude similarity and personal evaluation. *Bulletin of the Psychonomic Society*, *4(5)*, 479–481.

Bem, D.J. (1972). Self-perception theory. In L. Berkowitz (Ed.), *Advances in Experimental Social Psychology* (Vol. 6, pp. 1–62). New York: Academic Press.

Bennenbroek, F.T.C., Buunk, B.P., Stiegelis, H.E., Hagedoorn, M., Sanderman, R., Van den Bergh, A.C.M. & Botke, G. (2003). Audiotaped social comparison information for cancer patients undergoing radiotherapy: Differential effects of procedural, emotional and coping information. *Psycho-Oncology*, *12*, 567–579.

Bierhoff, H.W. (2002). *Prosocial behaviour*. London: Psychology Press.

Bierhoff, H.W. & Rohmann, E. (2004). Altruistic personality in the context of the empathy-altruism hypothesis. *European Journal of Personality*, *18(4)*, 351–365.

Boyar, S.L., Maertz, C.P. & Pearson, A.W. (2005). The effects of work-family conflict and family-work conflict on non-attendance behaviors. *Journal of Business Research*, *58(7)*, 919–925.

Breakwell, G.M. (2004). *Doing social psychology research*. Leicester: British Psychological Society.

Brehm, S.S., Kassin, S.M. & Fein, S. (2005). *Social psychology* (6th edn). Boston: Houghton Mifflin Company.

Brennan, A. & Kline, T. (2000). A justice explanation of employee reactions to office relocation: A case study. *Psychologist-Manager Journal*, *4(1)*, 105–115.

Brief, A.P., Dietz, J., Cohen, R.R., Pugh, D.S. & Vaslow, J.B. (2000). Just doing business: Modern racism and obedience to authority as explanations for employment discrimination. *Organizational Behavior and Human Decision Processes*, *81(1)*, 72–97.

Brodbeck, F.C. & Greitemeyer, T. (2000). Effects of individual versus mixed individual and group experience in rule induction on group member learning and group performance. *Journal of Experimental Social Psychology*, *36(6)*, 621–648.

Brug, J., Glanz, K., Van Assema, P., Kok, G. & Van Breukelen, G. (1998). The impact of computer-tailored feedback on fat, fruit and vegetable intake. *Health Education & Behavior*, *25*, 357–371.

Brug, J., Oenema, A. & Campbell, M. (2003). Past, present and future of computer-tailored nutrition education. *American Journal of Clinical Nutrition*, *77*, 1028–1034.

Brug, J., Van Vugt, M., Van den Borne, B., Brouwers, A. & Van Hooff, H. (2000). Predictors of willingness to register as an organ donor among Dutch adolescents. *Psychology & Health*, *15(3)*, 357–368.

Buunk, B.P. (1990). Affiliation and helping interactions within organizations: A critical analysis of the role of social support with regard to occupational stress. In W. Stroebe & M. Hewstone (Eds.), *European review of social psychology* (Vol. 1, pp. 293–322). Chichester: John Wiley.

Buunk, B.P., Bakker, A.B., Siero, F.W., van den Eijnden, R.J.J.M. & Yzer, M.C. (1998). Predictors of AIDS-preventive behavioral intentions among adult heterosexuals at risk for HIV-infection: Extending current models and measures. *AIDS Education and Prevention*, *10*, 149–172.

Buunk, B.P. & Bosman, J. (1986). Attitude similarity and attraction in marital relationships. *Journal of Social Psychology*, *126(1)*, 133–134.

Buunk, A.P. & Gibbons, F.X. (2007). Social comparison: The end of a theory and the emergence of a field. *Organizational Behavior and Human Decision Process*, *102*, 3–21.

Buunk, B.P., Gibbons, F.X. & Visser, A. (2002). The relevance of social comparison processes for prevention and health care. *Patient Education and Counseling*, *47*, 1–3.

Buunk, A.P., Massar, K. & Dijkstra, P. (2007). A social cognitive evolutionary approach to jealousy: The automatic evaluation of one's romantic rivals. In J. Forgas, M. Haselton & W. Von Hippel (Eds.), *Evolution and the social mind: Evolutionary psychology and social cognition* (pp. 213–228). New York: Psychology Press.

Buunk, B.P. & Schaufeli, W.B. (1999). Reciprocity in interpersonal relationships: An evolutionary perspective on its importance for health and well-being. *European Review of Social Psychology*, *10*, 259–291.

Buunk, B.P., & Verhoeven, K. (1991). Companionship and support at work: A microanalysis of the stress-reducing features of social interaction. *Basic and Applied Social Psychology*, *12(3)*, 243–258.

Buunk, B.P. & Ybema, J.F. (1997). Social comparisons and occupational stress: The identification-contrast model. In B.P. Buunk & F.X. Gibbons (Eds.), *Health, coping and well-being: Perspectives from social comparison theory* (pp. 359–388). Hillsdale, NJ: Erlbaum.

Buunk, B.P., Zurriaga, R., Gonzalez-Roma, V. & Subirats, M. (2003). Engaging in upward and downward comparisons as a determinant of relative deprivation at work: A longitudinal study. *Journal of Vocational Behavior, 62,* 370–388.

Byrne, D. (1971). The ubiquitous relationship: Attitude similarity and attraction: A cross-cultural study. *Human Relations*, *24(3)*, 201–207.

Byrne, D., Ervin, C.R. & Lamberth, J. (1970). Continuity between the experimental study of attraction and real-life computer dating. *Journal of Personality & Social Psychology*, *16(1)*, 157–165.

Campbell, D., Carr, S.C. & Maclachlan, M. (2001). Attributing 'third world poverty' in Australia and Malawi: A case of donor bias? *Journal of Applied Social Psychology*, *31(2)*, 409–430.

Cassel, B.J. (1995). Altruism is only part of the story: A longitudinal study of AIDS volunteers. *Dissertation Abstracts International: Section B: The Sciences and Engineering,* Vol. 56(5-B), pp. 2937.

Cialdini, R., Kallgren, C. & Reno, R. (1991). A focus theory of normative conduct: Theoretical refinement and re-evaluation of the role of norms in human behaviour. In L. Berkowitz (Ed.), *Advances in experimental social psychology* (pp. 201–234). San Diego, CA: Academic Press.

Cialdini, R.B. & Trost, M.R. (1998). Social influence: Social norms, conformity, and compliance. In D.T. Gilbert, S.T. Fiske & G. Lindzey (Eds.), *The handbook of social psychology* (Vol. II, pp. 151–192). Boston: McGraw-Hill.

Clarke, S., Botting, N. & Norton, M. (2001). *The complete fundraising handbook*. London: Directory of Social Change.

Cooper, C.L., Dyck, B. & Frohlich, N. (1992). Improving the effectiveness of gain-sharing: The role of fairness and participation. *Administrative Science Quarterly*, *37(3)*, 471–490.

Cooper, J. & Fazio, R.H. (1984). A new look at dissonance theory. In L. Berkowitz (Ed.), *Advances in experimental social psychology* (Vol. 17, pp. 229–266). New York: Academic Press.

Crandell, C.S. (1988). Social contagion of binge eating. *Journal of Personality and Social Psychology*, *55*, 588–598.

Daly, M. & Wilson, M. (2001). Risk-taking, intrasexual competition, and homicide. In J.A. French, A.C. Kamil & D.W. Leger (Eds.), *Evolutionary psychology and motivation* (pp. 1–36). Lincoln: University of Nebraska Press.

Darwin, C. (1871). *The descent of man and selection in relation to sex*. New York: D. Appleton and Company.

Dawes, R.M. & Messick, D.M. (2000). Social dilemmas. *International Journal of Psychology*, *35(2)*, 111–116.

Dawes, R.M., Van de Kragt, A.J. & Orbell, J.M. (1988). Not me or thee but we: The importance of group identity in eliciting cooperation in dilemma situations: Experimental manipulations. *Acta Psychologica*, *68(1–3)*, 83–97.

DiClemente, C.C., Prochaska, J.O., Fairhurst, S.K. & Velicer, W.F. (1991). The process of smoking cessation: An analysis of precontemplation, contemplation, and preparation stages of change. *Journal of Consulting and Clinical Psychology*, *59(2)*, 295–304.

Dijker, A.J., Koomen, W. & Kok, G. (1997). Interpersonal determinants of fear of people with AIDS: The moderating role of predictable behavior. *Basic and Applied Social Psychology, 19*, 61–79.

Dijkstra, A. (2005). Working mechanisms of computer-tailored health education: Evidence from smoking cessation. *Health Education Research, 20*, 527–539.

Dovidio, J.F., Piliavin, J.A., Schroeder, D.A. & Penner, L.A. (2006). *The social psychology of pro-social behavior.* Mahwah, NJ: Erlbaum.

Dutton, D.G. and Aron, A.P. (1974) Some evidence for heightened sexual attraction under conditions of high anxiety. *Journal of Personality and Social Psychology, 30*, 510–517.

Elander, J., West, R. & French, D. (1993). Behavioral correlates of individual differences in road-traffic crash risk: An examination of methods and findings. *Psychological Bulletin, 113(2)*, 279–294.

Evans, L. & Hardy, L. (2002). Injury rehabilitation: A goal-setting intervention study. *Research Quarterly for Exercise & Sport, 73*, 310–319.

Festinger, L. (1954). A theory of social comparison processes. *Human Relations, 7*, 117–40.

Festinger, L. (1957). *A theory of cognitive dissonance.* Oxford: Row, Peterson.

Fischer, P., Greitemeyer, T., Pollozek, F. & Frey, D. (2006). The unresponsive bystander: Are bystanders more responsive in dangerous emergencies? *European Journal of Social Psychology, 36(2)*, 267–278.

Fishbein, M. & Ajzen, I. (1975). *Belief, attitude, intention, and behavior: An introduction to theory and research.* Reading: Addison-Wesley.

Fishman, J.A. & Galguera, T. (2003). *Introduction to test construction in the social and behavioral sciences: A practical guide.* Lanham: Rowman & Littlefield.

Fiske, S.T. (1998). Stereotyping, prejudice and discrimination. In D.T. Gilbert, S.T. Fiske & G. Lindzey (Eds.), *The handbook of social psychology* (pp. 357–411). Boston: McGraw-Hill.

Fliszar, G.M. & Clopton, J.R. (1995). Attitudes of psychologists in training toward persons with AIDS. *Professional Psychology Research and Practice, 26*, 274–277.

Folkman, S., Lazarus, R.S., Dunkel-Schetter, C., DeLongis, A. & Gruen, R.J. (2000). The dynamics of a stressful encounter. In T.E. Higgins & A.W. Kruglanski (Eds.), *Motivational science: Social and personality perspectives* (pp. 111–127). New York: Psychology Press.

Gage, A.J. (1998). Sexual activity and contraceptive use: the components of the decision making process. *Studies in Family Planning, 29(2)*, 154–166.

Galanter, M., Hayden, F., Castañeda, R. & Franco, H. (2005). Group therapy, self-help groups, and network therapy. In R.J. Frances & S.I. Miller (Eds.), *Clinical textbook of addictive disorders* (3rd edn, pp. 502–527). New York: Guilford Publications.

Gardner, G.T. & Stern, P.C. (1996). *Environmental problems and human behavior.* Needham Heights: Allyn & Bacon.

Geurts, S.A., Buunk, B.P. & Schaufeli, W.B. (1994a). Health complaints, social comparisons, and absenteeism. *Work & Stress, 8*, 220–234.

Geurts, S.A., Buunk, B.P. & Schaufeli, W.B. (1994b). Social comparisons and absenteeism: a structural modeling approach. *Journal of Applied Social Psychology, 24*, 1871–1890.

Geurts, S.A., Schaufeli, W.B. & Buunk, B.P. (1993). Social comparison, inequity, and absenteeism among bus drivers. *European Work and Organizational Psychologist, 3*, 191–203.

Gibbons, F.X., Gerrard, M. & Lando, H.A. (1991). Social comparison and smoking cessation: The role of the 'typical smoker'. *Journal of Experimental Social Psychology, 27(3)*, 239–258.

Gillespie, R. (1991). *Manufacturing knowledge: A history of the Hawthorne experiments.* Cambridge: Cambridge University Press.

Graham, S., Weiner, B., Giuliano, T. & Williams, E. (1993). An attributional analysis of reactions to Magic Johnson. *Journal of Applied Social Psychology, 23(12)*, 996–1010.

Griffitin, W. (1970). Environmental effects on interpersonal affective behavior: Ambient effective temperature and attraction. *Journal of Personality and Social Psychology, 15(3)*, 240–244.

Guagnano, G.A., Stern, P.C. & Dietz, T. (1995). Influences of attitude-behavior relationships: A natural experiment with curbside recycling. *Environment and Behavior, 27(5)*, 699–718.

Hardy, C. & Van Vugt, M. (2006). Nice guys finish first: The competitive altruism hypothesis. *Personality and Social Psychology Bulletin, 32,* 1402–1413.

Heilman, M.E., Simon, M.C. & Repper, D.P. (1987). Intentionally favored, unintentionally harmed? Impact of sex-based preferential selection on self-perceptions and self-evaluations. *Journal of Applied Psychology, 72(1)*, 62–68.

Helweg-Larsen, M. & Collins, B.E. (1994). The UCLA Multidimensional Condom Attitudes Scale: Documenting the complex determinants of condom use in college students. *Health Psychology, 13(3)*, 224–237.

Hewstone, M., Stroebe, W. & Jonas, K. (2005). *Social Psychology* (4th edn). Oxford: Blackwell.

Hogg, M. & Turner, J.C. (1987). Intergroup behaviour, self-stereotyping and the salience of social categories. *British Journal of Social Psychology, 26(4)*, 325–340.

Hogg, M. & Vaughan, G. (2005). *Social Psychology* (4th edn). London: Prentice Hall.

Huhmann, B.A. & Brotherton, T.P. (1997). A content analysis of guilt appeals in popular magazine advertisements. *Journal of Advertising, 26(2)*, 35–45.

Jackson, D., Mannix, J. & Faga, P. (2005). Overweight and obese children: Mothers' strategies. *Journal of Advanced Nursing, 52(1)*, 6–13.

Joireman, J.A., Van Lange, P.A.M. and Van Vugt, M. (2004). Who cares about the environmental impact of cars? Those with an eye toward the future. *Environment and Behavior, 36(2)*, 187–206.

Karau, S.J. & Williams, K.D. (1993). Social loafing: A meta-analytic review and theoretical integration. *Journal of Personality and Social Psychology, 65(4)*, 681–706.

Kashima, Y., Gallois, C. & McCamish, M. (1993). The theory of reasoned action and cooperative behaviour: It takes two to use a condom. *British Journal of Social Psychology, 32(3)*, 227–239.

Kenrick, D.T. & Johnson, G.A. (1979). Interpersonal attraction in aversive environments: A problem for the classical conditioning paradigm? *Journal of Personality and Social Psychology, 37(4)*, 572–579.

Kenrick, D.T., Neuberg, S.L. & Cialdini, R.B. (2005). *Social psychology: Unraveling the mystery* (3rd edn). Boston, MA: Allyn & Bacon.

Kerr, N.L. (1989). Illusions of efficacy: The effects of group size on perceived efficacy in social dilemmas. *Journal of Experimental Social Psychology, 25(4)*, 287–313.

Kerr, N.L. & Tindale, S.R. (2004). Group performance and decision making. *Annual Review of Psychology, 55,* 623–655.

Kitayama, S., Markus, H.R., Matsumoto, H. & Norasakkunkit, V. (1997). Individual and collective processes in the construction of the self: Self-enhancement in the United States and self-criticism in Japan. *Journal of Personality and Social Psychology, 72,* 1245–1267.

Kiviniemi, M.T., Snyder, M. & Omoto, A.M. (2002). Too many of a good thing? The effects of multiple motivations on stress, cost, fulfillment, and satisfaction. *Personality and Social Psychology Bulletin, 28(6)*, 732–743.

Kline, G.H., Pleasant, N.D., Whitton, S.W. & Markman, H.J. (2006). Understanding couple conflict. In A.L. Vangelesti & D. Perlman (Eds.), *The Cambridge handbook of personal relationships* (pp. 445–462). Cambridge: University Press.

Kluger A.N. & DeNisi, A. (1998). Feedback interventions: Toward the understanding of a double-edged sword. *Current Directions in Psychological Science, 7(3)*, 67–72.

Kok, G.J., Schaalma, H., De Vries, H., Parcel, G. & Paulussen, T. (1996). Social psychology and health education. In W. Stroebe & M. Hewstone (Eds.), *European Review of Social Psychology* (Vol. 7, pp. 241–282).

Komorita, S.S. & Parks, C.D. (1994). *Social dilemmas.* Madison, IL: Brown & Benchmark.

Koslowsky, M. & Krausz, M. (2002). *Voluntary employee withdrawal and inattendance: A current perspective.* New York: Kluwer Academic/Plenum Publishers.

Kramer, G.P. & Kerr, N.L. (1989). Laboratory simulation and bias in the study of juror behavior: A methodological note. *Law and Human Behaviour, 13(1),* 89–99.

LaPiere, R.T. (1934). Attitudes versus actions. *Social Forces, 13,* 230–237.

Latané, B. & Darley, J. (1970). *The unresponsive bystander: Why doesn't he help?* New York: Appleton-Century-Crofts.

Lerner, M.J. (1980). *The belief in a just world: A fundamental delusion.* New York: Plenum Press.

Levy, S.R., Freitas, A.L. & Salovey, P. (2002). Construing action abstractly and blurring social distinctions: Implications for perceiving homogeneity among, but also empathizing with, and helping others. *Journal of Personality and Social Psychology, 83(5),* 1224–1238.

Lind, A.E. & Tyler, T.R. (1997). Procedural context and culture: Variation in the antecedents of procedural justice judgments. *Journal of Personality and Social Psychology, 73(4),* 767–780.

Linville, P., Fischer, G.W. & Fischhoff, B. (1993). AIDS risk perceptions and decision biases. In J.B. Pryor & G.D. Reeder (Eds.), *The social psychology of HIV infection* (pp 5–38). Hillsdale, NJ: Lawrence Erlbaum.

Locke, E.A. & Latham, G.P. (2002). Building a practically useful theory of goal setting and task motivation: A 35-year odyssey. *American Psychologist, 57,* 705–717.

Luzzo, D.A., Hasper, P., Albert, K.A., Bibby, M.A. & Martinelli, E.A. (1999). Effects of self-efficacy-enhancing interventions on the math/science self-efficacy and career interests, goals, and actions of career undecided college students. *Journal of Counseling Psychology, 46,* 233–243.

Lyas, J.K., Shaw, P.J. & Van Vugt, M. (2002). Recycling in a London borough: Perceptions, participation and barriers to the use of survival bags. Paper presented at the *Proceedings of Waste.* Stratford-upon-Avon, 24–26 September.

Lyas, J.K., Shaw, P.J. & Van Vugt, M. (2004). Provision of feedback to promote householders' use of a kerbside recycling scheme: a social dilemma perspective. *Journal of Solid Waste Technology and Management,* 30, 7–18.

Lyness, K.S. & Thompson, D.E. (2000). Climbing the corporate ladder: Do female and male executives follow the same route? *Journal of Applied Psychology, 85(1),* 86–101.

Lynn, M. & Mynier, K. (1993). Effect of server posture on restaurant tipping. *Journal of Applied Social Psychology, 23(8),* 678–685.

Lyubomirsky, S., Sheldon, K.M. & Schkade, D. (2005). Pursuing happiness: The architecture of sustainable change. *Review of General Psychology, 9(2),* 111–131.

Maio, G.R. & Esses, V.M. (1998). The social consequences of affirmative action: Deleterious effects on perceptions of groups. *Personality and Social Psychology Bulletin, 24(1),* 65–74.

Manstead, A.S.R. & Hewstone, M. (1995). *The Blackwell encyclopedia of social psychology.* Cambridge: Basil Blackwell.

Mantler, J.L. (2001). Judgements of responsibility for HIV-infection: A test of Weiner's social motivation theory in the context of the AIDS epidemic (immune efficiency). *Dissertation Abstracts International: Section B: The Sciences and Engineering, 61(9-B),* 5057.

Markus, H.R. & Kitayama, S. (2003). Culture, self, and the reality of the social. *Psychological Inquiry, 14(3–4),* 277–283.

Martin, C.L. & Brennett, N. (1996). The role of justice judgments in explaining the relationship between job satisfaction and organizational commitment. *Group & Organization Management, 21(1),* 84–104.

Martin, G. & Pear, J. (2003). *Behavior modification: what is it and how to do it.* Englewood Cliffs, NJ: Prentice-Hall.

McCalley, L.T. & Midden, C.J.H. (2002). Energy conservation through product-integrated feedback: The roles of goal-setting and social orientation. *Journal of Economic Psychology, 23*, 589–603.

McGuire, W.J. (1985). Attitudes and attitude change. In G. Lindzey & E. Arouson, *Handbook of social psychology* (pp. 233–346). New York: Random House.

Montada, L. (1992). Attribution of responsibility for losses and perceived injustice. In L. Montada, S.H. Fillip & M. Lerner (Eds.), *Life crises and experiences of loss in adulthood* (pp. 133–62). Hillsdale, NJ: Erlbaum.

Montada, L. (2001). Solidarität mit der Dritten Welt/Solidarity with the third world. In H.W. Bierhoff & D. Fetchenhauer (Eds.), *Solidarität: Konflikt, Umwelt, Dritte Welt/Solidarity: Conflict, Environment, Third World* (pp. 65–92). Opladen: Leske & Budrich.

Myers, D. (2005). *Social psychology*. Boston: McGraw-Hill College.

O'Keefe, D.J. (1990). *Persuasion: Theory and research*. Newbury Park, CA: Sage.

O'Keefe, D.J. (2002). *Persuasion: theory and research*. Thousand Oaks, CA: Sage Publications.

Omoto, A.M. & Snyder, M. (1995). Sustained helping without obligation: Motivation, longevity of service, and perceived attitude change among AIDS volunteers. *Journal of Personality and Social Psychology, 68(4)*, 671–686.

Omoto, A.M., Snyder, M. & Martino, S.C. (2000). Volunteerism and the life course: Investigating age-related agendas for action. *Basic and Applied Social Psychology, 22(3)*, 181–197.

Oskamp, S., Burkhardt, R.L., Schultz, W.P., Hurin, S. & Zelezny, L. (1998). Predicting three dimensions of residential curbside recycling: An observational study. *Journal of Environmental Education, 29(2)*, 37–42.

Oskamp, S. & Schultz, W.P. (2001). *Attitudes and opinions* (3rd edn). Mahwah, NJ: Erlbaum.

Ovretveit, J. (2001). *Action evaluation of health programmes and changes: a handbook for a user-focused approach*. Abingdon: Radcliffe Publishing.

Paulus, P.B. & Dzindolet, M.T. (1993). Social influence processes in group brainstorming. *Journal of Personality and Social Psychology, 64(4)*, 575–586.

Paulussen, T., Kok, G. & Schaalma, H. (1994). Antecedents to adoption of classroom-based AIDS education in secondary schools. *Health Education Research, 9*, 485–496.

Paulussen, T., Kok, G., Schaalma, H. & Parcel, G.S. (1995). Diffusion of AIDS curricula among Dutch secondary school teachers. *Health Education Quarterly, 22(2)*, 227–243.

Penner, L.A., Dovidio, J.F., Piliavin, J.A. & Schroeder, D.A. (2005). Find more like this prosocial behavior: Multilevel perspectives. *Annual Review of Psychology, 56*, 365–392.

Podell, S. & Archer, D. (1994). Do legal changes matter? The case of gun control laws. In M. Costanzo & S. Oskamp (Eds.), *Violence and the law*. Thousand Oaks, CA: Sage Publications.

Prislin, R. & Wood, W. (2005). Social influence in attitudes and attitude change. In D. Albarracín, B.T. Johnson & M.P. Zanna (Eds.), *The handbook of attitudes* (pp. 671–705). Mahwah, NJ: Erlbaum.

Quine, L. (2002). Workplace bullying in junior doctors: Questionnaire survey. *British Medical Journal, 324,* 878–879.

Reed, M.B. & Aspinwall, L.G. (1998). Self-affirmation reduces biased processing of health-risk information. *Motivation and Emotion, 22*, 99–132.

Reis, H.T. & Judd, C.M. (2000). *Handbook of research methods in social and personality psychology*. New York: Cambridge University Press.

Rogers, E.M. (1983). *Diffusion of innovations*. New York: The Free Press.

Rosenberg, M. (1965). *Society and the adolescent self-image*. Princeton, NJ: Princeton University Press.

Ross, L. (1977). The intuitive psychologist and his shortcomings. In L. Berkowitz (Ed.), *Advances in experimental social psychology* (Vol. 10, pp. 173–220). New York: Academic.

Rudolph, U., Roesch, S.C., Greitemeyer, T. & Weiner, B. (2004). A meta-analytic review of help giving and aggression from an attributional perspective: Contributions to a general theory of motivation. *Cognition & Emotion, 18(6)*, 815–848.

Rutter, D.R., Quine, L. & Albery, I.P. (1998). Perceptions of risk in motorcyclists: Unrealistic optimism, relative realism and predictions of behaviour. *British Journal of Psychology, 89(4)*, 681–696.

Schaalma, H., Kok, G. & Peters, L. (1993). Determinants of consistent condom use by adolescents: The impact of experience of sexual intercourse. *Health Education Research, 8(2)*, 255–269.

Schaller, M., Simpson, J.A. & Kenrick, D.T. (2006). *Evolution and social psychology*. New York: Psychology Press.

Schultz, P.W. & Oskamp, S. (2000). *Social psychology: An applied perspective*. Upper Saddle River, NJ: Prentice-Hall.

Schwartz, S.H. (1977). Normative influences of altruism. In L. Berkowitz (Ed.), *Advances in experimental social psychology* (Vol. 10, pp. 221–279). San Diego, CA: Academic.

Sheeran, P., Abraham, C. & Orbell, S. (1999). Psychosocial correlates of heterosexual condom use: A meta-analysis. *Psychological Bulletin, 125(1)*, 90–132.

Sheeran, P. & Silverman, M. (2003). Evaluation of three interventions to promote workplace health and safety: evidence for the utility of implementation intentions. *Social Science & Medicine, 56*, 2153–2163.

Sheeran, P. & Taylor, S. (1999). Predicting intentions to use condoms: A meta-analysis and comparison of the theories of reasoned action and planned behavior. *Journal of Applied Social Psychology, 29(8)*, 1624–1675.

Sheeran, P., Webb, T.L. & Gollwitzer, P.M. (2005). The interplay between goal intentions and implementation intentions. *Personality and Social Psychology Bulletin, 31(1)*, 87–98.

Sherman, D.A.K., Nelson, L.D. & Steele, C.M. (2000). Do messages about health risks threaten the self? Increasing the acceptance of threatening health messages via self-affirmation. *Personality and Social Psychology Bulletin, 26*, 1046–1058.

Silver, R.C., Wortman, C.B. & Crofton, C. (1990). The role of coping in support provision: The self-presentational dilemma of victims of life crises. In B. Sarason, I. Sarason & G. Pierce (Eds.), *Social Support: An international view* (pp. 397–426). New York: Wiley.

Skinner, B.F. (1956). A case history in scientific method. *American Psychologist, 11*, 221–233.

Smith, K.H. & Stutts, M.A. (2003). Effects of short-term cosmetic versus long-term health fear appeals in anti-smoking advertisements on the smoking behaviour of adolescents. *Journal of Consumer Behaviour, 3*, 157–177.

Smith, P.K., Talamelli, L., Cowie, H., Naylor, P. & Chauhan, P. (2004). Profiles of non-victims, escaped victims, continuing victims and new victims of school bullying. *British Journal of Educational Psychology, 74*, 565–581.

Sparks, P., Shepherd, R., Wieringa, N. & Zimmermans, N. (1995). Perceived behavioural control, unrealistic optimism and dietary change: An exploratory study. *Appetite, 24(3)*, 243–255.

Steadman, L. & Quine, L. (2004). Encouraging young males to perform testicular self-examination: A simple, but effective, implementation intentions intervention. *British Journal of Health Psychology, 9*, 479–487.

Steiner, I.D. (1972). *Group process and productivity*. New York: Academic Press.

Strecher, V.J., Seijts, G.H., Kok, G.J., Latham, G.P., Glasgow, R., DeVellis, B., Meertens, R.M. & Bulger, D.W. (1995). Goal setting as a strategy for health behavior change. *Health Education Quarterly, 22,* 190–200.

Stroebe, W. & Stroebe, M.S. (1995). *Social psychology and health.* Belmont: Brooks/Cole Publishing Co.

Stürmer, S., Snyder, M., Kropp, A. & Siem, B. (2002). Empathy-motivated helping: The moderating role of group membership. *Personality and Social Psychology Bulletin, 32(7),* 943–956.

Sunnafrank, M. (1992). On debunking the attitude similarity myth. *Communication Monographs, 59(2),* 164–179.

Sutton, S.R. & Eiser, J.R. (1984). The effect of fear-arousing communications on cigarette smoking: An expectancy value approach. *Journal of Behavioral Medicine, 7,* 13–33.

Swann, W.B., Stein-Seroussi, A. & Giesler, R.B. (1992). Why people self-verify. *Journal of Personality and Social Psychology, 62,* 392–401.

Taylor, P.J., Russ-Eft, D.F. & Chan, D.W.L. (2005). A meta-analytic review of Behavior Modeling Training. *Journal of Applied Psychology, 90,* 692–700.

Thibaut, J.W. & Kelley, H.H. (1959). *The social psychology of groups.* New York: Wiley.

Thompson, L.L. (2006). Negotiation: Overview of theory and research. In L.L. Thompson (Ed.), *Negotiation theory and research* (pp. 1–6). Madison: Psychosocial Press.

Tyler, T.R. & Blader, S. (2002). The influence of status judgments in hierarchical groups: Comparing autonomous and comparative judgments about status. *Organizational Behavior and Human Decision Processes, 89,* 813–838.

UNAIDS/WHO (2005). *Aids epidemic update 2005.*

Van Baaren, R.B., Holland, R.W., Steenaert, B. & Van Knippenberg, A. (2003). Mimicry for money: Behavioral consequences of imitation. *Journal of Experimental Social Psychology, 39(4),* 393–398.

Van Lange, P.A.M. & De Dreu, C.K.W. (2001). Social interaction: Cooperation and competition. In M. Hewstone & W. Stroebe (Eds.), *Introduction to social psychology* (pp. 341–370). Oxford: Blackwell.

Van Vugt, M. (1998). The conflicts in modern society. *Psychologist, 11(6),* 289–292.

Van Vugt, M. (1999). Solving natural resource dilemmas through structural change: The social psychology of metering water use. In M. Foddy, M. Smithson, S. Schneider & M. Hogg (Eds.), *Resolving social dilemmas: Dynamic, structural, and intergroup aspects* (pp. 121–133). New York: Psychology Press.

Van Vugt, M. (2001). Community identification moderating the impact of financial incentives in a natural social dilemma: Water conservation. *Personality and Social Psychology Bulletin, 27(11),* 1440–1449.

Van Vugt, M. (2006). Evolutionary origins of leadership and followership. *Personality and Social Psychology Review, 10,* 354–371.

Van Vugt, M., De Cremer, D. & Janssen, D. (2007). Gender differences in competition and cooperation: The male warrior hypothesis. *Psychological Science, 18,* 19–23.

Van Vugt, M., Meertens, R.M. & Van Lange, P.A.M. (1995). Car versus public transportation? The role of social value orientations in a real-life social dilemma. *Journal of Applied Social Psychology, 25(3),* 258–278.

Van Vugt, M. & Samuelson, C.D. (1999). The impact of personal metering in the management of a natural resource crisis: A social dilemma analysis. *Personality and Social Psychology Bulletin, 25(6),* 731–745.

Van Vugt, M., Snyder, M., Tyler, T. & Biel, A. (2000). *Cooperation in modern society: Promoting the welfare of communities, states, and organizations.* London: Routledge.

Van Vugt, M. & Van Lange, P.A.M. (2006). Psychological adaptations for prosocial behavior: The altruism puzzle. In M. Schaller, D. Kenrick & J. Simpson (Eds.), *Evolution and social psychology* (pp. 237–261). New York: Psychology Press.

Van Vugt, M., Van Lange, P.A.M., Meertens, R.M. & Joireman, J.A. (1996). How a structural solution to a real-world social dilemma failed: A field experiment on the first carpool lane in Europe. *Social Psychology Quarterly, 59(4),* 364–374.

Verplanken, B. & Aarts, H. (1999). Habit, attitude, and planned behaviour: Is habit an empty construct or an interesting case of automaticity? *European Review of Social Psychology, 10,* 101–134.

Walker, F.H., Taylor, A.J. & Green, D.E. (1990). Attitudes to AIDS: A comparative analysis of a new and negative stereotype. *Social Science & Medicine, 30(5),* 549–552.

Walker, I. & Smith, H.J. (2002). *Relative deprivation: Specification, development, and integration.* New York: Cambridge University Press.

Watson, D., Clark, L.A. & Tellegen, A. (1988). Development and validation of brief measures of positive and negative affect: The PANAS scales. *Journal of Personality and Social Psychology, 54(6),* 1063–1070.

Weiner, B. (1990). Searching for the roots of applied attribution theory. In S. Graham & V.S. Folkes (Eds.), *Attribution theory: Applications to achievement, mental health, and interpersonal conflict* (pp. 1–13). Hillsdale, NJ: Erlbaum.

Weiner, B. (1993). AIDS from an attributional perspective. In J.B. Pryor & G.D. Reeder (Eds.), *The social psychology of HIV infection* (pp. 287–302). Hillsdale, NJ: Erlbaum.

Weiner, B., Perry, R.P. & Magnusson, J. (1988). An attributional analysis of reactions to stigmas. *Journal of Personality and Social Psychology, 55(5),* 738–748.

Weinstein, N. (2003). Exploring the links between risk perceptions and preventive health behavior. In J. Suls & K. Wallston (Eds.), *Social psychological foundations of health and illness.* Malden: Blackwell.

Weinstein, N.D. & Klein, W.M. (1996). Unrealistic optimism: Present and future. *Journal of Social & Clinical Psychology, 15(1),* 1–8.

Wheeler, L. & Suls, J. (2005). Social comparison and self-evaluations of competence. In A.J. Elliot & C.S. Dweck (Eds.), *Handbook of competence and motivation* (pp. 566–578). New York: Guilford Publications.

WHO (2005). http://www.unaids.org/eu/HIV_data/epi2006/

Wood, J.V., Taylor, S.E. & Lichtman, R.R. (1985). Social comparison in adjustment to breast cancer. *Journal of Personality and Social Psychology, 49,* 1169–83.

INDEX